Love Changes Everything

Love Changes Everything

David Icke

Aquarian/Thorsons
An Imprint of HarperCollins*Publishers*

The Aquarian Press
An Imprint of HarperCollins*Publishers*
77–85 Fulham Palace Road,
Hammersmith, London W6 8JB

Published by The Aquarian Press 1992
1 3 5 7 9 10 8 6 4 2

A catalogue record for this book
is available from the British Library

ISBN 1 85538 247 4

Printed in Great Britain by
HarperCollinsManufacturing Glasgow

To the Spirit of the Earth

A brighter dawn awaits the human day,
When poverty and wealth, the thirst of fame,
The fear of infamy, disease and woe,
War with its million horrors and fierce hell,
Shall live, but in the memory of time.

Percy Bysshe Shelley

Contents

Acknowledgements 11

Introduction 13

1. The Way, theTruth, and the Light 17
2. In the Beginning 31
3. The Crystal Wonderland 42
4. The Fallen Angel 55
5. Living in the Light 74
6. The Great Divide 97
7. The Family 109
8. The Plan 128
9. Lady of Love 152
10. New World 159

Acknowledgements

I would like to thank Linda, Mari, Joan, Kerry and Gareth for their love and support, and the many thousands of people who have sent messages of love and support. Thank you to Mari for her wonderful channelling, and to Joan for her work in checking the text through her own psychic communications with the higher levels of Creation. My thanks, also, to all those on the light levels who care for us, guide us, and communicate the information.

Introduction

March 29th, 1990, was the day my life changed in the most extraordinary way. At that time I was a television presenter and a spokesperson for the United Kingdom Green Party. My life was full, secure, and constantly challenging. Or so I thought.

That spring morning I visited a medium and spiritual healer to be treated for rheumatoid arthritis, and a world opened up before me that has led to ridicule, condemnation, and some sadness, yes, but also to immense challenges, satisfaction, wonder and joy, as the treasures of Creation have been revealed to me. Through this medium I was contacted by those on the unseen levels of life who are guiding the Earth and her people through a transformation that will change the face of this planet and the attitudes and behaviour of all life-forms. A world beyond our dreams awaits us after the turmoil of transition is over and the glorious truths are known and accepted by everyone.

The communications said that I would bring these truths to public attention in books and through the media, and I have. My first book, *The Truth Vibrations*, told of these early days and of the spiritual awakening that is within the potential of all people. I was led to many sensitives and psychics in Britain and other countries, and through them the Godhead and other beings of vast evolution have unveiled to me the mysteries of life. All have told of the same events to come in this decade, the great geological upheavals that will bring an end to the pain and suffering, anger and conflict that have taken this planet to the brink of non-existence. They have made it clear also that the time of change that is needed to bring this about will be tough.

This second book, *Love Changes Everything*, reveals why this must happen, how we can cope, and the peace, love and harmony that will be ours just a few years from now. Since the publication of *The Truth Vibrations* I have learned so much more as I have communicated almost daily with Rakorski, the one known as Lord of all Civilization, who is directly responsible for the changes the Earth will undergo. I also communicate often with the one we know as Jesus, the Spirit of the Earth, and many others. This may sound fantastic and beyond belief, and I can understand that. It is hard to take in from the limited perspective that imprisons humanity. But I hope that by the time you have finished reading this book you will appreciate that communicating with such beings on other levels of Creation is the most natural thing in the world. Everything is a living spirit. A flower, a tree, an insect, an animal, a human, a planet – all have within their physical form a living, thinking spirit. Why then is it so astonishing to so many that we can communicate with them?

Every time we think we create energy, a *thought-form*, as it is called. A thought-form has no language as such, it is just a thought, an energy field which can be decoded by others into any language they like. This is how telepathy works. A thought-form sent out by an Italian will be decoded by an Englishman into English, by a Frenchman into French. In this way thought-forms sent to us by the Spirit of the Earth or by a being from another part of the universe can be decoded into spoken words by someone with psychic gifts which, indeed, all of us possess. This is called *channelling*. The thought-forms are decoded by an area of the brain close to our other listening devices, the ears.

This decoding can manifest in many ways, not only through the spoken word. The thought-forms can be turned into written words, and this is known as *automatic writing*. Your hand writes on the paper, sometimes with incredible speed, but the words and the information are not yours and could not possibly be yours, because you often know nothing about the subject taking shape in front of you. It is also possible to hear the thought-forms as a soft, gentle voice inside your head. I call this method 'getting it direct'. On a more limited level it is possible to communicate through *dowsing*. This is when a pendulum swings one way for 'yes' and another for 'no'.

All these methods have been used to accumulate and check the information for *Love Changes Everything*, and the overwhelming majority of the channelling has been done by a colleague, Mari Shawsun. Through Mari, many others, and my own communications I have been able to speak at great length since early 1990 with those who are helping the planet and humanity through this crucial period in their evolution. They have asked me to put together in this book all that I have learned so far, and to write the story of Creation and the Earth in a way that will explain why we are in the position we are today and what we can do about it.

If we are to reduce the fear and confusion that these geological events will bring, it is essential that people know what is going on and why. Only by understanding how we reached this point can we really appreciate why the upheavals are an act of love by the Spirit of the Earth and not some kind of vengance for the way she has been treated. If these events were not to happen there would be no planet and no humanity by the middle of this decade, if not before, the channellings have said.

You will see the word *love* many times, because it is the rock on which Creation is founded. Everything is energy, and the most powerful energy is love. This love is so different to the one we have come to understand; it is not romantic, soppy or showy. It does not seek to possess or own another. Nor is it limited by condition. A love that says 'I love you when' or 'I love you if' is no love at all. True love knows no boundaries, no conditions. It is given freely and equally to all, with nothing expected or demanded in return. It is an energy we can receive from each other and from every level of Creation, and with our thoughts of love we can send this energy out to others and to the environment in which we live. This is the love that can and will change everything.

Although there is a large amount of new and detailed information in this book, the basic foundations of what you will read have also been channelled by endless psychics over many centuries, and others on Earth today are receiving information which supports much of what I say. Even so, as I have said many times, I do not ask or urge you to believe a word of it. That is your choice, and everyone's choice is to be respected.

If, however, you are ready to open your heart and mind, the confusions of life are about to be unravelled. You will realize who you really are; you will see that there is no death, only eternal life and eternal love. You will receive guidance from the highest sources in Creation as you reassess your thoughts and beliefs in the light of geological and human events; and you will, I so sincerely hope, begin to see that there is nothing to fear.

You are special, because every life-form in Creation is equally special. You were created with equal thought and love, and as this reality finds its place in human understanding the trials of this physical life will lift and disperse. Love will change everything, the love you give and the love you receive. The truth that has eluded humanity for so long is about to be set before you. It is a truth that will change your life and change this world forever.

David Icke
Ryde,
Isle of Wight
November 1991

1.

The Way, The Truth and the Light

The information in this book is the result of many hundreds of hours of channelling, and it has been a mighty task to work through it, check it again and again, and pick out the areas most relevant at this great time of change.

I have written the story in chronological order, with particular emphasis on the last 12,000 years, during which time the events began which have brought us to where we are today. The last two chapters will then concentrate on the present and how we can act to help ourselves and the planet. There will be occasions when I need to break off from the main narrative to explain certain things which are essential to know if people are to understand what will follow. It is for this reason that I will start with a brief summary of the founding principles of Creation:

The Levels of Life

Everything is energy. The wall of your house, the ground beneath your feet, your own physical body – all are made of energy vibrating at different speeds. These different speeds are called *frequencies* or *vibrations*. Nothing is solid as such. If you look through a microscope at something that seems solid you will see that it is merely vibrating energy. When this universal energy vibrates at other speeds the less solid the substance appears, and when it is vibrating at a certain speed it can no longer be seen by the human eye. Most of Creation is invisible to us because it is vibrating at speeds too fast for our eyes to see, and this has helped fuel the myth that Creation is limited only to what we can see, touch, feel or smell. In truth what we can perceive is but a tiny, tiny fraction of all that is.

This is why we cannot see all the other life-forms of Creation. They operate on different frequencies, beyond our ability to see. Some people get an idea of this principle when they see a 'ghost'. It is quite correct that the psychically sensitive can see spirits float through walls and the like. The frequency of the wall is so different to that of the spirit that the spirit can pass through it, in the same way that radio waves pass through the walls of buildings to be picked up by the transistor. If one frequency of vibration could not pass through another you wouldn't be able to use a radio indoors, because the sound waves would not be able to get into the house!

Creation is made up of a series of energy frequencies. These are the levels of life. On the Earth we live on a very low frequency, and this is why we can see so little of Creation. The higher the frequency, the more knowledge, wisdom, understanding and ability to love is available to us. It is no surprise that humanity has found it so hard to appreciate the truth about Creation, given the low frequency on which we operate.

When Jesus said 2,000 years ago, 'In my father's house there are many mansions', he was speaking of these frequencies of life. Think of a radio with its many frequencies. You tune the dial to one wave length frequency and you get that radio programme and no other. The same principle applies to all Creation. At any one time we are 'tuned' by our stage of evolution to a particular frequency, and that is our home until we evolve through experience and learning to a higher frequency or fall as a result of imbalance to a lower one. These frequencies are not piled on top of one another like a chest of drawers. They extend throughout Creation, and share the same space. Think of them as files in a filing cabinet, with each one lying against, rather than on top of the others. This is possible because different frequencies can exist in the same space without being aware of each other. Witness all the frequencies of radio stations, television stations and telecommunications equipment around you now. You can't see them and are not aware of them, but they are all existing in the space around you. Tune in with the right technology and there they are. Move the dial and one disappears, to be replaced by another.

Each higher frequency contains the sum total of all the knowledge and experience accumulated on that frequency and on all those below, but it does not have access to the knowledge and experience on frequencies higher than itself. This is because those on the lower frequencies would not be able to understand the wealth of knowledge existing on the higher frequencies. As we evolve we progress to ever more wonderful levels of life, but if we fall down the frequencies we have access to less knowledge, wisdom, understanding and ability to love. This is why it has become so difficult for the truth of Creation to be accepted by humanity since 'the fall of man'. This biblical term really means the fall down the frequencies, and it has had disastrous consequences for the Earth and Creation as a whole.

Within each frequency band are sub-frequencies, or *sub-planes* as we will call them. Imagine a ladder, with the space between each rung representing a frequency. Now think of a series of little rungs between the main ones. These are the sub-planes, and we climb these until we reach the top of the frequency and move up to the next level. People may be together on one overall frequency, but they will be at different stages of evolution, on different sub-planes, within that frequency. You would see a big contrast in the behaviour, understanding and wisdom of those on the highest and lowest sub-planes of the same overall frequency – the evidence of this is all around us on Earth today. Some people seek conflict, others seek peace.

It is, however, necessary to emphasize that Creation is not a hierarchy or league table with those on the higher frequencies dictating to those below. Nor is it the case that those on higher frequencies are considered 'better' beings. To be evolved is merely to have used experience to gain wisdom. It is not to be perfect, and the higher you go the further you have to fall if you are affected by certain experiences. The most highly evolved beings can have unpleasant experiences and react to them in a less than balanced way. No one likes to fall down the frequencies, but it can lead to greater learning and help you to evolve even more quickly as a result. There are those who choose to experience the lower frequencies in order to learn from situations that are only available there; for the same reason there are others who decide to stay on a frequency when they could move up. There are no hard-and-fast rules, only personal choices. No matter where we are on the frequencies we are all equal and no one is considered superior to anyone else. We are guided equally and loved equally, whoever we are and whatever we do.

Our True Identity

Each frequency of life has a physical level and a non-physical or *light level*. The light level is our natural home, and we come into physical bodies for learning experiences that help to speed our evolution through greater understanding and wisdom. The real us is not the physical body we see – that is just a highly sophisticated shell we use for learning experiences. It has great limitations compared with how we live on the light levels, and this makes it a very effective vehicle for learning. On the light levels in our non-physical spirit form we can travel anywhere instantly merely by thought, and we can see the truth of Creation far more clearly than we can while in a physical body.

The real us is this non-physical spirit form. We are created by thought-form energy. There are those thought-forms that send out messages which other sensitive people can decode, as I have explained, and then there is another type of thought-form, which can be used on the higher levels to create life. This kind of thought-form has such power that it gathers energy particles together within the 'parent' being and from the environment to create another living entity. This new being stays within the parent until it has reached the stage where it can operate independently. In simple terms it is like a baby growing within the womb.

When a being is created it is no more than a beam of energy with a series of spinning 'wheels' or vortexes of energy within the beam. These spinning wheels of energy are called *chakras*. The higher your frequency the more you have. On the physical level of this frequency we have seven. The chakras are highly sensitive and have the power to do many wonderful things, as you will see as we go along. If you relate them to the physical body they are positioned at the base of the spine (base chakra), in the sex organs (sacral chakra), the solar plexus (solar plexus chakra), the centre of the chest near the heart (heart chakra), the throat (throat chakra), the forehead (third-eye chakra), and on top of the head (crown chakra). They are linked to the physical body through the endocrine system. Most people can't see them because they are part of the real us, our spirit or light bodies, and not the physical. When I talk of chakras I mean the main ones, because there are smaller versions around the body also.

The Godhead was created in the same way as all other beings are created, and so we are told, quite rightly, that man was created in God's image. Not physical man, because that is a shell the spirit takes on for certain experiences. Man is created in God's spiritual image, the chakras and the beam of light.

Once this core being emerges from the parent, it creates for itself several other levels. It uses thought-power to gather together a series of energy fields or 'aspects'; these are called the spiritual, emotional, mental and etheric aspects, which I will be explaining in more detail later. Enough to say for now that these aspects are there to help the core being, the chakras and the beam of light, to experience most effectively on its journey towards balance and evolution. Energy flowing through the chakras is passed on to these other aspects continually, and all are working as one. It is this amalgamation of energy aspects and the chakra core that together make up the being that we really are. This amalgamation of levels working together is called a *light being* or whole being. The Bible calls it the soul. When it is created a light being is a babe in arms in evolutionary terms, and it then begins to experience, learn and grow. As it does so, the chakras spin quicker and more efficiently, and are able to draw in and use more energy. This makes the beam of light larger, and increases the light being's power and potential.

A light being is neither male nor female, but a combination of both. We only use male and female physical bodies to experience certain situations and energies. On the light levels we are both male and female. In the absence of a good term to describe a male/female I will use he/she and similar descriptions. However, there are some beings who are dominated by male or female energies, or who are working predominantly with one or the other as a learning experience. I will refer to them as he or she as appropriate. What matters is that we remember that our eternal, spirit self is both male and female.

Progress up the Frequencies

To progress to ever more wonderful levels, we need to find the balance of negative and positive energies within us. Energy flows through the chakras, so making them spin. The more balanced the energy between negative and positive the quicker they spin, and the quicker they spin the quicker the entire light being vibrates – its frequency goes up. When they are spinning fast enough the being can move up to the next level of life as the frequencies become compatible. So to progress up the frequencies, whether you are the Godhead or on the lowest level, you need to find the balance between negative and positive energies by having negative and positive experiences. When you reach that perfect balance of energies, a third energy is created which makes the chakras spin at the speed necessary to take us up from one frequency to another. It is this 'third force' that all of us are trying to produce by balancing negative and positive energies within the chakras. Once you reach the next frequency the process of seeking positive-negative balance starts again at the new level, until the third force is again produced.

The Law of Karma

Karma is one method through which this balance and third force can be achieved. Every thought and action creates positive or negative energy. It is vital, if we are to understand Creation, to appreciate that every thought creates energy. Those of hate, anger, resentment, fear, etc. create extremely negative energy, or negativity, as it is called, while those of love, forgiveness, caring, sharing, etc. produce positive energy. So as we experience positive and negative situations and thoughts, the equivalent energies flow through the chakras and are absorbed by our light being. The law of karma is there to help us balance out these experiences and therefore balance the negative/positive energies within us. It also helps us to enjoy a balance of experiences and knowledge, which leads us in the most efficient way to wisdom and understanding. We have countless physical incarnations, and we come into each of them with a life-plan designed to give us the negative and positive experiences we feel we need to find a balance of both energies and knowledge.

Under this system of karma a negative experience needs to be balanced by a positive experience of, in an ideal situation, equal power in terms of energy. This is what is meant by 'What you sow, so shall you reap,' and is also the meaning behind the biblical phrase 'An eye for an eye, a tooth for a tooth.' It means that what we do to others will need to be done to us to balance out the experiences. The best advice we can have is 'do unto others as you would have them do unto you.' Terrorists, for example, are really only terrorizing themselves, because they will need to experience what they have done to others to balance out their experience and understanding, just as those who hate and abuse people for their colour or beliefs will need to experience that same action done to them to help their journey to balance and progress up the frequencies. It doesn't necessarily have to be done immediately. It could be thousands of physical lifetimes before the opportunity arises to experience what we have made others experience, but it will need to happen at some point if we wish to progress.

It is important to stress that no one is judged for his or her behaviour, except by him- or herself, and that there is no judgemental God pointing out wrong-doings and forcing us to take the appropriate punishment. Free will is the foundation of all Creation. All life-forms are free to make their own decisions and their own choices, to find their own balance in their own way and in their own time. There is endless guidance available – 'ask and you shall receive', but no compulsion. In Creation the choices are ours and ours alone. The only way possible, however, to find the balance of energies and the necessary knowledge is by a balance of experiences, and if there is to be progress up the frequencies to ever greater wisdom and love, then karma is the only way to achieve it.

Finding this balance has an enormous effect on our thinking, attitudes and behaviour. When we are out of balance in the positive direction this shows itself in certain characteristics. At its most extreme we float away in some sort of spiritual daze, and love turns to idolatry and worship. We lose touch with the practical side of life. If we are out of balance to the negative extreme we desire to dominate and control, and hatred, anger and conflict ensue. This is the situation we have on the Earth today.

When all imbalances are corrected we enjoy the benefits of the best characteristics of positive and negative energies. With positive this includes the ability to love everyone equally without condition, to care without being affected by emotion, to share without expecting anything in return, to forgive and accept, to be compassionate, to have understanding and empathy, to communicate with the higher levels of light, to serve with a generosity of spirit, to have inner security and peace and to gain wisdom through learning.

Negative energies include the ability to have discipline, to organize, to be determined, to strive to get things done, to stimulate the body and mind to overcome problems, to be proud of achievements, to have a sense of justice and fairness, and to seek equality and a sense of fellowship. You can see that the word 'negative' as humans have come to understand it is very different from its true meaning. Negative energies are just as necessary as positive, and a problem only arises when one dominates the other. The greater the domination, the greater the imbalance and the more extreme the problem. On the other hand, when we find the balance between the two, life becomes so much easier.

Balancing energies to rise up the frequencies is not the sole reason for karma. It is also about personal development. Only through sufficient experience, knowledge and wisdom will we be able to live usefully on a higher level. It is a little like going up to a higher class in a school when you are not developed enough to absorb and understand the information set before you. You can walk in the door and sit at the desk, but will you be able to understand what is going on around you? Karma offers the route to wisdom and understanding that allows us to operate successfully on a higher frequency.

The Light

This word has been used so liberally by the religions of the world, but no satisfactory explanation or definition has been forthcoming. It has nothing to do with daylight. The Light is an energy which is produced by the highest source in Creation and sent out to every life-form. It is the perfect balance of negative and positive energies, and is created with the most powerful positive energy of them all – love. It is the lifeforce of Creation. The Light also carries information. All the knowledge, experience and wisdom that every life-form has amassed is absorbed by the highest source and passed on to Creation. The energy that carries this information is the Light. If we receive the Light it makes it so much easier to find the balance we need to progress.

The lower our frequency, the less powerful is the Light, and the more imbalanced the frequency the more the Light is weakened. Again, this is the case on this planet today. The frequency of the Light and other energies need to be reduced to match each frequency of life. If they reached us at their original power we would be fried. It would be like walking into the most powerful laser beam. The further you are away from a radio transmitter, the weaker the signal, and the same is true of the Light. This is why we have access to more knowledge, understanding and wisdom the higher we rise up the frequencies. The higher we go the more powerful is the Light, and so the more information is available to us. This information helps us to see who we really are and where we wish to go. This in turn gives us a better understanding of karma and how it can be used to speed our evolution.

I should make it clear that although the Light is weaker on the lower frequencies it is still there to be used, and within our own beings we carry all the information we need to operate successfully on this level. It is just a matter of tuning in to that information within us, and the Light can help us to do this. The best way is to sit quietly, listen, and ask to be tuned in to the Light.

Other Energies

Every life-form and every object carries and generates energies. We all have our own personal energies that are unique to us. They are like spiritual fingerprints, and they are created from the sum total of all our experiences. The energy flow through the chakras brings energies to us and picks up our experiences and knowledge, balances or imbalances, and sends them up through energy lines to the higher frequencies. The chakras also generate these energies out into the world around us, and if our energy systems are imbalanced we send imbalanced energies to our own environment. These imbalances are then absorbed by the spirit of the planet and all those who live on the surface. When you walk into a room or a building you can often feel the energies that have been generated there. The atmosphere may feel unpleasant, eerie, aggressive or happy, and on these occasions you are feeling the energies, negative and positive, around you. If most people are sending out imbalanced energies the whole planet can become imbalanced. This is what has happened to the Earth.

Every life-form in Creation operates on the same principle. The stars and planets are the physical bodies of thinking, feeling, reacting, spiritual beings of high evolution. They also have a series of chakras and a beam of light working with the other aspects, the spiritual, emotional, mental and etheric. Like us, they too have unique personal energies which they generate, and this is the basis for astrology. Their energies influence us in different ways; the nearer a planet is to this one in its cycle the more powerful are the energies we receive. Those energies also include the ones that a planet receives from other sources and those generated by all the life-forms on and within that planet. If you can work out in detail the planets that will most influence the Earth with their energies at a given time, you can predict likely behaviour patterns, although these planetary energies only have the power to influence us and no more. The power of our free will always allows us to reject those influences if we so choose.

Even objects which appear lifeless have energies. They have the energies of those who created them and of those who have touched them or been close to them, particularly the people who have owned them for a long time. They also carry the energy from the substances they are made of, the energies they have absorbed from the atmosphere, and the energies generated by the thoughts behind their creation. For instance, a tank, a gun or any weapon will carry negative energies even if it is never used. Its function and reason for existence is negative, therefore so are its energies. It is the same with concrete and tarmac, pesticides, nuclear plants, the internal combustion engine, and all the other substances and machines that are used to poison the Earth with man-made misunderstanding. All pollution carries and generates negative energy, as does everything created through the abuse and misuse of the Earth's resources. Every time we cut down a tree or pick a flower we are cutting short the physical life of that being and it is no wonder that negative energy is produced. Everything that portrays a negative or positive experience, such as a film, picture or news report, also generates that same energy. Think about this paragraph for a moment and apply it to the world's political, military, economic, industrial and communication systems. Imagine how much negative energy is created and generated every minute of every day from these sources alone.

Words also carry the thought energy that created them as well as the energy generated by whatever they say and stand for. The titles of my books, *The Truth Vibrations* and *Love Changes Everything*, carry such energies. *The Truth Vibrations* is an appropriate title because it has a vibration that helps people to understand the truth. *Love Changes Everything* has an energy that will help the reader to understand love, cope with change, and appreciate the wholeness of Creation. You can see that we are subject to the influence of a limitless number of energies from near and far, and all have an effect on the energy system and the behaviour patterns of the Earth and every life-form upon her. We live in a sea of energy and we are all like droplets of water in the ocean, individual to an extent, but all part of the whole.

The Energy System

All stars, planets and life-forms are linked together by the energy network that spans Creation. You could think of these energy lines as arteries carrying the blood supply, in this case energy, to all life-forms. It is a network of energy lines that begins at the highest source and brings the Light and other energies down the frequencies. This network links up with a planet's own energy system. If you could see the Earth from the Light levels you would see a sort of spider's web of energy lines – ley lines, some people call them – which picks up all the energies generated and carries them to every part of the planet. Each being absorbs energies and generates his or her own, so what we do on Earth is passed on through this network to all Creation. We are all responsible karmicly for the energies we generate, because they affect the whole.

Channelling Energies

I have talked about the channelling of information, but the channelling of energy is different. You will hear this term many times, so an early explanation is required. When you channel while in a physical body you receive energies through your hands and all the main chakras. The chakras then go to work to produce the required mixture of energies, and sometimes to reduce the frequency to one which the Earth can absorb. When this has been done – and it takes only a few seconds – the energy can be released through the heart, base, and crown chakras, and through the hands and feet. It is also possible to receive energies and then, by thought, project them long distances to an area without necessarily needing to go there physically. The energies can be used in a variety of ways to heal the Earth, diffuse negativity where necessary, and generally boost the energy system. Channelling from the light levels follows the same principle, using the chakras to mix the energies and reduce the frequency before passing them down the appropriate energy lines. It is necessary for those in physical bodies to channel and bring in those energies a planet may at certain times need above and beyond those that normally come down the lines, or when, as in the case of the Earth today, many of the lines linking her with the overall grid have been severed. There are a great many people doing this work during this period of change, under guidance from the light levels. Spiritual healing, or the 'laying on of hands', is also a form of channelling, as energies are passed through a healer to the patient.

There you have all the founding principles on which Creation is built and through which all life-forms evolve. I will go into them in more detail as we progress, but now, with the basic structure established, the story of Creation, and particularly of this planet, can begin.

I would ask you, however, to be selective and trust your own judgement. The information in this book is not mine, it has come through many channellings. I have merely written down this information in an order and sequence. Accept what feels right and have no qualms about rejecting what does not. Everything must rest with our personal judgement and belief.

2.

In the Beginning

'Let there be light and there was light' is a simple summary of how Creation began. There was a burst of energy from which all has evolved over periods of time we could not begin to comprehend, and it has brought us the glorious and ever-expanding haven of life and love in which we all live forever more.

The limitations of human language have made it difficult for those who have communicated this information. The true wonder and magnitude of Creation have always eluded humanity since spoken language was developed, and it is no surprise, therefore, that words do not exist to describe adequately how it all began. Rakorski, the one who is known as Lord of all Civilization, said:

> We are attempting to convey a basic outline of the start of Creation. Many will have further questions and feel a need to seek continually until they find the answers. As the frequencies rise more knowledge will be available to you, but as we watch your planet it is clear that such understanding could not manifest itself until the Great Time of Change and the new era is upon you. Then you will know many things and have the power to use your knowledge very wisely. Until then, my friends, listen to this amazing story of love and understanding and seek guidance from the light levels as you look for answers. The power is within you and all around you. It is the power of love.

In the beginning there was a void, a vacuum. Into this void appeared a nucleus of perfectly balanced energy, the Light. This energy had the ability to multiply itself. Hard as it may be to appreciate from our human perspective, this perfectly balanced, pure energy, could think and create. The energy itself produced energy, and so could expand in a never-ending, self-perpetuating process. The energy created energy, which created more energy and so on. The energy grew and expanded out into the void and reached the point where the mass had grown so large that the sum total of its ability to think and create was enough to evolve into a being at the centre core from which the energy was continually self-creating. This being is known to us as the Beyond, a being which, in effect, created him/herself.

You can imagine Creation as a little like those spinning fireworks we know in Britain as Catherine Wheels. At the centre was the Beyond, and around this being the Light energy was spinning in an ever-larger circle as more was produced. It is the same today. The outer borders of Creation are only limited by how far the Light spreads outwards into the void, in other words by how much light or lifeforce is produced. As the Beyond observed, learned, and evolved, he/she moved on to the next stage by creating another being through thought. This was not part of a grand plan, but the natural progression as the Beyond went in search of what was possible. This second being we will call the Guiding Godhead. The Beyond's knowledge and learning was greatly increased by this second being, because the Guiding Godhead's experiences could also be absorbed by the Beyond through the energy links between them.

In time, the Guiding Godhead wished to introduce a similar situation for him/herself and so created a third being, which we know as the Godhead. The more beings that are created, the more experiences and choices are produced as they interact with each other, and so the more potential there is for learning and evolution.

These were the three beings from which Creation has grown.

The Beyond is at the highest level, then comes the Guiding Godhead, followed by the Godhead. It is interesting to note that the Bible uses alternatively the terms Almighty God, Lord God and God the Father. The Bible sees them as one being when they are in fact three. The Almighty God is the Beyond, the Lord God is the Guiding Godhead, and God the Father is the Godhead.

The Beyond is at such a high level that the energies he/she produces and absorbs are perfection. They are exactly balanced and pure, and the two energies of negative/positive are as one. There is no need to seek balance, it is there, built in. The further you go down the frequencies the more there is a division of the energy into the two forms, negative and positive. So there is a need on the frequencies below that of the Beyond to seek a balance between the negative and positive energies as they flow through, and accumulate in, our beings.

The Beyond and the Guiding Godhead could see the potential for learning on the lower frequencies as beings searched for balance, and the creation of the Godhead was designed to put this process in motion. The Godhead would be responsible for guiding the frequencies below him/herself and for creating beings who would experience this challenge and pass on their experiences to the whole so that all would evolve. Until this point all experience had been on the non-physical, light levels, where life is so much easier than when we are subject to the limitations and challenges of a physical shell. I am not saying that life in our purely spirit form on the light levels is always easy, but it is easier.

The Godhead decided to create a being that would take on a physical body, because this offered enormous learning opportunities. There was also a need for the being to separate into two parts, as there is with all physical incarnations. The potential for learning may be high when we incarnate into a physical shell, but so is the potential for severe imbalance if we are unable to cope with its limitations. If the whole being incarnated under these circumstances the whole being would be severely imbalanced. Instead the Godhead decided that only part of the being would enter a physical body. The rest would stay on the light levels and act as a guide to support the incarnated part. Our energies can merge and separate at will, and this was the time when the principle of the 'higher self' (that remaining on the spirit frequencies) and 'lower self' (that which enters a physical body) came into operation. The higher self would communicate with the lower self through thought-forms, and this was another development that added to the learning opportunities presented by physical incarnation.

This evolutionary first was a big success, and the Godhead created six similar beings who also entered physical bodies, as planets. They worked and interacted, so enjoying even greater potential for free-will choices, positive and negative. The Godhead created beings to incarnate onto these planets, including the being known as Rakorski, and as time went on others became creators of life-forms as they progressed to a high enough level of wisdom and understanding. The expansion of Creation was now well under way. Every form of life was created with enormous thought, care, love and guidance from the highest levels. All were created for a reason and this continues to this day. It is most certainly not a case of 'I fancy creating a new being today!'

Rakorski has told us of his/her many lives on one of these first seven planets. He/she remembered how there were many giant crystals on the surface and an animal not unlike our horse. There were spirits for the crystals, the rocks and minerals, water, animals and light beings. A little later came the plant spirits. The same principles applied to all of them as they incarnated into their particular type of physical body.

The seven planets made up the first solar system as they rotated around the first sun, or *Solar Logos*. The Solar Logos is the spirit of a sun who guides a solar system and sends certain energies to the planets and stars. Very slowly and with great care

Creation expanded as the first universe (this one) was formed out of groups of solar systems, each guided by a Solar Logos. A universe is formed once a certain level of experience and evolution has been attained. When a being reaches an immensely high level of understanding and wisdom he/she becomes the overall guide for a group of solar systems, and that grouping is called a universe. The overall guide in this universe is known to us as *Altimar* – the being who incarnated into that first planet. Indeed the seven universes we currently have are all guided by those who were the spirits of the original seven planets.

As the expansion of Creation continued it was necessary to link up all the planets and stars with the lines of light coming down from the Beyond, and a vast grid network of lines was developed. The more evolved the planet spirit, the bigger, more vital the role he/she has in working with the energies before passing them on down the lines to the next planet. As this became more and more complex the Godhead decided to introduce many new forms of evolution. One has become known as the *deva* or angelic evolution. Among the many roles of the devas is to be guardians of the energy lines and sites, and to try to ensure that the grid works efficiently. They also have another important task. As is true of everyone in a physical body the spirit of a planet eventually disincarnates at the end of one learning period, and the physical planet dies. When that happens the devas step in to take over that planet's contribution to the energy system at a minimum level, until another spirit arrives to form a new planet at the same point on the grid. Without the guardianship of these spiritual 'repairmen' the system could not continue to operate.

The devas/angels have a different kind of free will to that of a light being in that they have an in-built wish to serve and support others and help them with their evolution. They also have a gift for understanding the energy system from the start, but their responsibility increases as they evolve. When they move up the frequencies they can become archangels. The most famous and evolved archangel in this universe is the Archangel Michael. The deva evolution has since widened its scope, and they now incarnate into physical bodies to experience the learning opportunities this offers. The ones known as the disciples at the time of Jesus were all devas.

So there you have the basics of how Creation began and evolved, but I am sure one particular question will have come to mind. How did that nucleus of perfectly pure Light first appear and start off this process of Creation? Are you ready for this? It was put there by another being that came before all I have described. This is the one called 'the Infinite Being. It has been made clear to me that it is simply not possible on this frequency to explain who and what this being really is, except that he/she is everything. All I can do is pass on to you how this being was described for us in a communication from Rakorski:

> The Infinite Being is a being of no beginning and no end. The Infinite Being has all wisdom, all truth, all understanding, and great love. The Infinite Being watches, observes and has no need for learning and experiencing because he is everything and everything is him/her. There are no impurities, no imbalances, only the ultimate in all that is, ever was, and ever will be. The Infinite Being had no reason for providing the energy that created the Beyond other than a love for creation. That is all.

For this book, at least, that is where we shall leave our attempts to understand and explain the nature of this astonishing being. OK, so the next question is who created the Infinite Being? We could go on and on like this, but the concepts would defy our ability to comprehend them at this stage of evolution on this frequency of life. And anyway, it is not what we need to know and understand at this crucial time. What we need to appreciate urgently is why we are in the situation we are today and what we can do about it.

We require an understanding of why the expansion and

evolution of Creation took such a sudden and potentially catastrophic turn, and central to this is planet Earth. Rakorski and the Spirit of the Earth were once the same being. Together as one they progressed up the frequencies as they learned and experienced from thousands of lives on many planets in many situations. Rakorski told us:

> We went to different planets to learn of healing, or conflict, or love. We gathered information, just as all beings do, which enabled us to receive the energies in larger quantities, because we wished to move up the frequencies. Our journey went eventually into other universes. There were some disappointments, of course, but we were really on the crest of a wave. It was so easy to be guided and we just seemed to fly higher. The great imbalance of Creation had not occurred, and though our negative experiences might bring tears or an act of unkindness, they never reached to the extremes of today.

The Godhead sent out a thought-form inviting the very highly evolved being Earth Spirit/Rakorski to separate as a learning experience for all. One half would work through the physical body of a planet with an extremely important task to perform, and the other would guide her from the light levels. The two beings became known as Rakorski and the Earth Spirit, and their energy patterns balanced and complemented each other perfectly. Rakorski said:

> We were very delighted – it was such an honour, such a privilege. There was tremendous excitement. We didn't know how long it would be or how it would turn out. But on the light levels, where you see and know so much more, such a thought-form caused great excitement and elation that we were being given the opportunity to love Creation and show this so positively.

The Earth Spirit was to experience female energies in this incarnation as part of her life plan, so I will use female terms for her and male for Rakorski, to avoid endless he/shes. But again we

need to remember that both of them are male and female. Such
was her stage of evolution that the Earth Spirit was one of the
most evolved planet spirits in all Creation. This was necessary,
because her role in Creation's energy system was to be a vital
one. She was to be the harmonizing planet for this universe.
Harmonizing means healing. The energies passing through the
Earth are harmonized, balanced between negative and positive.
The Earth Spirit and all the crystals, rocks, minerals, etc. also
add their own unique energies to the mixture. These energies are
then passed on down the lines to the universe. They help other
planets and life-forms heal themselves physically, emotionally,
mentally and spiritually. They carry the lifeforce, stimulate the
re-growth of tissue cells, and unblock energy lines. When either
negative or positive energies are dominant this can cause
blockages in the lines, a little like the blockages in the arteries of
a physical body.

If these healing energies are weakened or removed it is much
more difficult to check imbalances before they reach the serious
stage of runaway, self-perpetuating imbalance which can send a
planet plummeting down the frequencies. There is a planet in
each of the seven universes which has the role of harmonizer, but
if this system breaks down the imbalance to one universe will
affect other universes because everything is connected.
Rakorski's task was to guide from the light levels, pass on to the
Earth the energies from the Godhead plus his own energies, and
come to the planet in a physical body as necessary to channel
various other energies. Before the Earth Spirit incarnated to
begin her role as the harmonizer for the universe there was
another planet spirit at this point on the energy system who was
harmonizing the energies. Eventually this spirit decided she had
learnt as much as was necessary in that incarnation and chose to
disincarnate to continue her journey of learning elsewhere. After
many experiences this spirit is back in this solar system as
another planet . . . she is the Spirit of Venus.

The Earth was created with enormous thought and care,

because harmonizing the energies is of immense importance. The Godhead used all the knowledge absorbed since Creation began to put together this magnificent work of art called planet Earth. The Earth Spirit has channelled information to us about this time:

> The Godhead knew which of the substances he had ever created would be most appropriate for helping this planet function according to his/her plan. The land was extremely varied because of its many functions. All the components have very important roles. Every type of 'fossil fuel' or crystal or mineral was put into this planet because it would make a contribution to the harmonizing energies that I would transmit out to the universe. I have always marvelled at the structure of my physical body. Everything on this planet has a purpose, everything makes a contribution to the whole.

> I cannot explain the way in which all these substances were put together to make this spinning ball. With each thought from the Godhead something new was created and put into place. It was a swirling mass of this thought energy for a long time, but gradually it took shape and became my physical body. Give or take a few thousand years, this all happened 45 billion years ago. [About 40 billion years earlier than human science has believed.]

I stress again that only part of the being we call the Earth Spirit incarnated into the physical body. As with all physical incarnations, most of the being (the higher self) stayed on the light levels to support and guide the part that incarnated (the lower self). The land on the new planet was created in a way that allows it to be moved and changed in structure very easily. This can happen in periods when a planet progresses to a higher frequency or needs to re-balance her energies, and are known as the 'physical changes'. We are going through such a period today. The physical body of a planet may need to be changed in this way for several reasons: (1) When a planet moves up a frequency the energy system might need to change considerably and the make up of the land may have to be rearranged to ensure the necessary rocks and substances are in the correct place to match the new energy network (2) It might also be necessary to change the balance of land and water. (3) It is an opportunity to remove negative or positive imbalances by releasing the appropriate energies from within the planet through volcanoes and landshifts and bring to an end the way of life that is causing the imbalance. (4) There may be a need to move around the various substances that make up the planet, the crystals, rocks and minerals, etc., and to change their quantities. A period of enormous physical change always ends with an axis shift because there is a need to balance out the Earth's electro-magnetic field within and around the planet with the new energy system and frequency. There were many such changes in the early stages of this planet's life.

So the Godhead had given birth to a new and spectacular planet, and the Earth Spirit began her task of harmonizing the energies. Many beings were very keen to come here once things had begun to settle down after that first million years, and there has been 'life' on Earth, as humans term it, for nearly 45 billion years! The Earth Spirit said:

> It was soon open house. It is funny, I often laugh when I hear your men of science. They think 500 million years is very old. I hear the great excitement and delight as scientists discover new things, new creatures, how people lived, what they looked like, but they are discovering things that are so recent. I could make their eyes pop out if I could show them past civilizations that have lived on this planet.

Many beings and creatures came and went in different physical bodies with different ways of living and different thinking patterns. All were at a high level of evolution because only those who were on or above, the Earth's frequency could exist here. This meant the Earth was treated with respect. The population was also nothing like as large as it is today. All her inhabitants understood the Earth's chakra and energy systems and the role she played in the universe.

Civilizations rose and declined. Sometimes it was with only minimal effect, other times immense physical changes took place before these civilizations reached their natural conclusion and ended. Usually all evidence of their existence disappeared. This was either because evidence could not manifest as the Earth reached a higher frequency or because it became buried deep within the Earth during the landshifts.

As this process continued the Earth Spirit was having negative and positive experiences, finding balance and moving up the frequencies. As the frequencies rose some life-forms could no longer manifest here, among these were the dinosaurs, who disappeared over thousands of years because of the quickening vibrations and physical change. Then around 50,000 years ago came the civilization called Lemuria, later shortened to Mu. I will refer to it throughout as Mu for the sake of consistency. It was known that the Earth Spirit was preparing to move up to a higher frequency, and so a large number of beings arrived hoping to experience enough and learn enough to go with her. They hoped that if they could spend time among the Earth Spirit's energies and the Godhead energies that were harmonized by this planet they would find the same balance that she and Rakorski enjoyed and could go with them to the higher frequency.

Most of these beings did not manage to follow the Earth Spirit up to the next frequency on this occasion, but a few did. After the geological changes that brought in the new frequency it was they, and many who came from other planets, who began the Muan civilization.

3.

The Crystal Wonderland

The Muan lands covered a large area of the planet, and the population numbered around a billion at its peak. They were a very pleasant, gentle people. They could make sounds, but they communicated mostly through telepathy. Remember we are talking about people working on a much higher frequency than we know today, and so much more was possible.

They knew the energy system, and in the earlier period of their civilization they worked with the Earth Spirit by channelling to her certain energies from the higher frequencies as she needed them. The Muans were small, very pale, and had little hair. They had thin bodies and very small hands. Their eyes looked sunken because of their high cheekbones. They wore white, and had long gowns made of a soft material which was a little like silk but much heavier. And they wore a bracelet and ring made of a substance now buried deep within the Earth and not discovered by the modern world. The nearest we have to it is white gold, and it was the Muans' symbol of infinite love.

A good lifespan for a Muan was, wait for it . . . about 500 years! It is worth explaining here how this was possible and will be again. When we incarnate into a physical body there is within our spirit being a certain amount of the lifeforce energies needed for our physical body to exist. This means that without absorbing any of the energy flowing through us we could still exist for a short time. Once this lifeforce is used up the physical body dies.

The more evolved you are the more of this lifeforce energy you have available to bring into physical incarnation, and so the longer, potentially, you can live. What really matters, though, is how efficiently your system absorbs the energy constantly passing through you to replenish that initial supply of lifeforce. Also, the more balanced you are the purer are the energies you absorb. So add together an evolved being incarnating with a large supply of lifeforce, an efficient chakra system and a relatively balanced energy mix and you have the potential to live for hundreds of years. Even when the imbalance occurred in the Muan civilization it was nothing like as severe as today, and only slightly affected their physical life expectancy. Physical lives will always need to end so we can go on to other experiences, but there is no reason, except for massive imbalance on many levels, why they should be as short as they are now.

The Muans were a placid people. They had tremendous respect for the Earth Spirit and the spirits of the land resources, called land spirits, especially those of the rocks. Much of their civilization was based on working with the energies of rocks, which they used for many purposes. When they constructed a building they would use the rock that generated the type of energy most suited to the purpose of the building. They were on a frequency in which they could manifest and de-manifest rock or matter through thought and sound. Everything is a frequency, and it is possible to change that frequency and later return it to its original one. This is how they could, in conjunction with the rock spirit, use thought-power to change the speed of a rock's vibration until it ceased to be 'solid'. They would then move this non-physical energy to wherever they wished and then return it to its original vibration – that of the physical rock. They could transport rocks of any size any distance in this fashion.

They were in such awe of the Earth Spirit and the land spirits that they started to become imbalanced in the direction of positive energies. As I said earlier, this shows itself when love and respect turns to worship and obsession. You sort of fly off in a daze of love and devotion and forget about the practical side of life. Their buildings were dedicated to these spirits, and the gigantic stone statues on Easter Island, 2,300 miles off the South American Coast, are the images of the most evolved land spirits worshipped by the Muans.

This information about Mu was given to us by the being known as Wang Yee Lee, his name from an incarnation in China 1200 years ago. Long before this he was also a Muan. Wang was the one who first communicated with me in 1990, and is part of the Rakorski team which is guiding us all through the current changes. Wang outlined how this imbalance of positive energy led the Muans astray:

> They felt so in awe of the spirits of the rocks and were so grateful that they dedicated the buildings to them. And the amount of rock used in various buildings was sometimes large enough to allow the spirit of the rock to live in the building. Well this was not their purpose or at all advisable. If the spirit of the rock lived in a building, who was going to continue the work that was required for harmonizing the Godhead energies? Some spirits were moved a very long way, which really made a mess of the energy system, and this jeopardized the harmonizing of the energies.

> As time passed, true understanding of the energy system was lost because the Muans had transported vital sites from their correct locations to places near to them. They did this because they wished the land spirits to always be close, something they thought would bring them closer to the Earth Spirit. This type of love and admiration was completely misguided, and there grew from all this a belief that those who had constructed these temples that contained the land spirits had also constructed a new energy system. This was incorrect. They had really created a mess.

Their energy imbalance had also weakened their links with the light levels, and they could not be guided back on course. The energy system became more complicated, and great ceremonies of worship to the land spirits and the Earth Spirit took precedence over any useful channelling of energies. It grew to ridiculous proportions. The energy system was in such a muddle that it threatened the Earth Spirit's ability to harmonize, and she decided to act to bring Mu to an end. A planet spirit is also there as a guide to all life-forms on and within her surface. This is part of her task. You can see that under this system it is quite natural for a planet spirit to communicate with her life-forms and offer guidance or explain what is going to happen and why. If there comes a point when it is necessary to take action to maintain balance for everyone's benefit and check the imbalances that are harming the progress of all in her care, then it is her duty to act. Sometimes this can mean enormous changes have to take place, but it is always done out of love and necessity, not malice.

The geological events that saw the end of Mu were gradual, over a period of about ten years. As you will see in due course, it is possible for the Earth Spirit to organize such changes so that tidal waves, landshifts and volcanoes scatter and move the rocks and minerals to the places they need to be. All the land that was Mu was submerged by the tidal waves, except for what are now called the Galapagos Islands and Easter Island, which is why those statues have survived.

These physical changes helped the Earth Spirit to achieve balance again, and she was ready to progress to the highest frequency she had yet achieved. This was the start of Atlantis. When the Earth's surface had settled down at the end of Mu, an area of land had appeared in what is now the Atlantic Ocean. It was almost surrounded by water, but with a narrow link to what became North America. The American continent, north and south, was then smaller and a different shape to what it is today. Rakorski came from the light levels with a number of other evolved beings to create this new and wondrous civilization.

A being known as Magnu, a former Atlantean and one of the Rakorski team, channelled most of the communications which described this period and the emergence of Atlantis. He said there were mountains made of crystals surrounding Atlantis, and that they formed a large basin in which the civilization began. There were four energy points around this basin, which formed a diamond of brilliant white energy, and an area in the centre made of emeralds. It was a glorious place, and soon it was the talk of all Creation. The new race of Atlanteans had many visitors from other planets all over the different universes, because news travelled far and wide of this beautiful, shining land that was to be a real treasure on the surface of this most evolved planet. It was a landmark in the evolution of the Earth, and I will describe Atlantis in some detail because this is the lifestyle that awaits us again after the transformation is complete.

The Atlanteans were very tall, an average of around 6 ft 5 in. They were graceful, with long faces and necks, slender shoulders and long, strong legs. Their hands were large but gentle, and, like the Muans, they had quite pale skins, almost translucent. As they went up the frequencies with the Earth Spirit, their eyes became much bluer and clearer and their skin seemed to glow white. They could see the auras (the energy bodies) of those around them as well as those of the crystals. They were calm and peaceful people, and their energy systems were so balanced and efficient they could live for around 700 years, although this fell to about 600 when imbalance set in. Their power of thought was strong, as was their ability to decode thought-form energy, so they had no spoken language.

Their bodies were much lighter and less dense than ours, and they were designed to live without solid food. They absorbed energies from the water and the environment. Their digestive systems were there to mix the energies, which would combine together to work within their bodies. As humanity has fallen down the frequencies so have we developed the need for solid food. The digestive system, as with the whole physical body, has changed dramatically. 'The different organs are no longer built to last,' Magnu said, 'And you are very delicate creatures!'

The animals also lived off the energies in water and their

environment. There was no law of the jungle in which animals killed each other, nor was there any exploitation of them by humans. Today the animal kingdom is founded on fear, but on the frequency of Atlantis humans viewed animals, and animals viewed each other, with love and mutual respect. In the new world after the changes this will be so again. Rakorski said:

There were fewer species of animal and birds and creatures of the water. Those that existed were free to live as they wished. We communicated with the animals through thought transference. We had species like your elephants and dolphins. These are very gentle, loving creatures, and even today if you look into the eyes of your descendents of these creatures you can see they carry a knowledge that is beyond human understanding. Our elephants were bigger and their tusks curled more at the ends. Some of the species were a sort of sandy-brown colour. The dolphins were also bigger. There were also many creatures, big and small, of the air. Your humming bird is very like a little bird we had, but most creatures were so different I find it hard to describe them. They were all so graceful, gentle and brilliant in their colours, and they made a sort of music, a sound that filled the air with harmony. Life was very natural, very gentle.

The climate was gentle, also. The axis then was more or less straight up, and while there were seasons they were not very varied. The Earth moved in such a way around the Sun that the climate was balanced. There were no dry areas, and the Earth Spirit guided all weather systems so that the Atlanteans did not experience extremes of hot and cold.

The most evolved Atlanteans, who were at the top of the frequency band, could pass through 'gateways' to meet and communicate with those on the light levels. At the gateways there existed a sort of half-way house between the light and physical levels. This is what is known as the Astral Plane. Here the physical beings could meet with their higher selves and their guides to discuss how their plan for that physical life was proceeding and what needed to be done to support the Earth Spirit. The gateways appeared as a circle of light, half below ground and half above, so all that the Atlanteans could see was a semi-circle or archway of light. They would stand in the centre and walk through to the Astral Plane. Every frequency has an Astral Plane between the physical and light levels, but only on much higher frequencies than ours can it be used in this way.

Rakorski and many others started Atlantis, and the population grew rapidly to thousands and then millions, to reach a high of around a billion. Some travelled to other areas and settled for certain periods in what are now the states of Arizona and Montana in the USA, and they set up a key energy site on the land that has become Central Park in New York City. There were also Atlantean energy sites and settlements in areas that are now Denmark, Russia, Austria, Italy, Luxor in Egypt, and North Africa. Later they set up energy sites in other places, such as Ayers Rock and Olga Rock in Australia and in Peru.

The most evolved Atlanteans travelled by thought. They would think of where they wished to go and would de-manifest themselves and then re-manifest at their destinations in the sort of 'beam me up, Scotty' fashion of *Star Trek*. The less evolved could do the same, but only between certain points on the energy lines. Others would travel along the energy lines at quite a speed without de-manifesting. The thoughts necessary to de-manifest need to be very powerful, as Magnu outlined:

> It is the power of the will. 'I will' is very positive. It is still a thought, but that statement 'I will' carried the necessary energy. But of course we never said 'I might' or 'I would like to' or 'maybe,' because we knew what we were doing. 'I will' was part of our everyday thought-language.

The first Atlanteans manifested themselves as adults when they came to Earth, but within a short time children were being born. Physical intercourse was very different to the way it is perceived by most people today. It was seen as a divine act, and given tremendous respect. The Atlanteans understood the scale of evolution that was necessary to create a being on the light levels, and they considered it a great honour to create on the physical. There was no pain during childbirth. It was very easy, relaxed and beautiful, and involved lights, water and serene music. Intercourse only happened when two people wished to create a child. Magnu said:

Today . . . [sexual intercourse] . . . is seen as some self-pleasing act. Many Atlanteans loved each other in a way that is impossible to describe, not just members of the opposite sex, but of the same sex as well. The positive energy of pure love was generated between the heart chakras and the hands and from the top of the head, and this is where we are going again.

There was no need for closed doors, and exclusion of anyone else was in any case impossible on that frequency. It was a wonderful place to be. I felt so content and so loved. There has been nothing like it for a very long time, and my heart aches for I long to bring such a wonderful place back to this planet, and I am so glad it is going to happen because we are not going backwards any more.

On the low frequency we have on Earth now we do not understand the true meaning of love. In Atlantis, as on the light levels, beings were happy enough owning themselves and their identity, they did not seek or wish to own others or be owned by others. Magnu said many had constant companions through a life, but the principle of marriage was never even considered.

Why would anyone want a piece of paper and a different name? These beings understood their identity. They did not require anything else. Such an act would be of total irrelevance and contribute nothing. I created many children with a number of women, and we had no need for anything other than that act because I loved each of them equally. They also loved each other, and many had children with other men.

We had no need of possessions, no family name was required, and the idea of a family tree containing all the people born or married into a family simply did not exist.

There was no purpose to such trivial pursuits. I owned my identity, my plan for that life, and that was so satisfying I did not need to own another being or a house or anything. It just did not happen and could not happen on such a frequency.

The Atlanteans required no sleep except when they wished to travel in light body. When the physical body is at rest, the light body can leave and travel on the astral level to other planets or wherever it wishes to go. Enough energy is left behind to keep the physical body ticking over at a minimum level while asleep. People continue to do this today, and it is called light body or astral travelling. The difference with the Atlanteans was that when they woke up they could remember everything about their light body journeys. Most people on our frequency either remember nothing, get a confused version which appears to have been a weird dream, or, at best, can remember a little of what happened. There is always an energy link, a sort of umbilical cord between the physical and light bodies, and when the physical shows signs of waking up the light body returns instantly. This is why we are often a little shocked when we wake up suddenly. In those circumstances our light body has just returned to the physical again in a fraction of a second!

Around and above the whole planet during Atlantis was the *Roof of Light*. This was a mirror image of the energy system on the ground, and created more energy in itself. Actually, mirror is a good analogy. If you direct energy at a mirror that energy is doubled. You have the original energy and that created by its reflection. When we look in a mirror there are suddenly two of us, the original and the reflection, and the Roof of Light worked on the same principle. The energy in the ley lines were reflected in the Roof of Light, and twice the energy was created in the area between the two. The Roof of Light could also project energy out from the Earth to the universe and the Godhead. It was the Atlanteans' way of returning in the best way they could the Godhead's love for them. They were making available their surplus energy so the Godhead could make it available to the rest of Creation.

The civilization worked closely with the energies of crystals, the most evolved spirits of rock and mineral evolution. The crystals were used to receive energies sent to the Earth from many sources and to generate down to the Earth Spirit energies that she required to achieve balance and continue to progress. The Earth moved up the frequencies several times during Atlantis, and such was the harmony between Atlanteans and the Earth that there was no need for massive physical changes to move from one level to another. There was no serious imbalance to clear away before the new frequency could be introduced, and the energy system was so well looked after it could move from old to new very smoothly. A communication from the Earth Spirit said:

> We were so evolved that there was no need to remove negativity in such a manner. The negative energy was usually dispersed by the being who had created it as soon as he or she realized what had been done. Our understanding of karma and free will was part of everyday life. Therefore our reactions to others were natural, yet well thought out. Our concern was not for the way others reacted to us, but how we reacted to them, because we understood karma.

There were areas in Atlantis where these truths were learned. Many writers have called them temples, but this makes them sound like places of religious worship, which was not the case. They were areas where those who were a little out of balance would go to be shown how their thoughts and actions affected others. The energies created in these areas gave each being the gift of 'sight,' so they could see the energies. They would be shown how negative energy could be produced by thought, and what an effect it had. It was all part of the process of helping everyone understand and achieve balance.

Atlantis was a fantastic civilization, and it is hard to comprehend that it all happened on the same planet we inhabit at the present time, when comparatively the crudest of technology is described as 'advanced' or 'state of the art'. Here was the most wonderful success story that evolution on the physical level had seen, a story of advancement up frequency after frequency during most of the period of Atlantis. One smooth step up the ladder of life followed another, and it didn't seem possible that such an advanced people could become significantly imbalanced. Eventually, however, they did. It didn't begin to compare with the imbalance we have today, but it was enough to check the progress of both the Earth and her life-forms.

There came a time when a few of the most evolved beings became a little over-proud of their achievements. They taught many other Atlanteans and worked hard for the energy system, but they allowed themselves to become a little conceited. They felt they were very important to the whole civilization, and started to set themselves apart from the rest. They marked out an area for themselves, and from that small beginning the rot set in. Hierarchy was born. It had always been accepted that some beings knew more than others, and that all could benefit from their knowledge, but they were never treated as superior. Everyone had the same rights, respect and lifestyle. The principle of equality began to crumble when the hierarchy was formed and the marking off of boundaries led to ownership and possession.

The intention behind these actions was not so much for self-glorification but more to emphasize that all beings could rise to the higher level. It was felt that by having a definite demarcation between those who were most evolved and others it would motivate everyone to try harder to evolve and join those most evolved. What it did, in fact, was create a system of 'us and them' which produced pride, resentment and division. This stimulated negative thought-energy, and imbalance began to roll. It was the start of the journey back down the frequencies.

This is how the split in Atlantis occurred, and as it did so the energy system and the Roof of Light became less powerful. The Earth Spirit decided, with guidance from Rakorski and the Godhead, that rather than see such wonderful people continue to fall down the frequencies she would create the physical changes that would end Atlantis. Those who were still balanced enough to listen to guidance from the light levels would be led to places of safety during the changes. They would later return to restore the Roof of Light and take the planet still further, to even higher frequencies than she had yet reached. You can see that the Earth Spirit did not make this decision out of anger or resentment. Her motivation was love, just as it is today. Had she done nothing, these beings who had worked so hard to evolve up the frequencies would have continued to fall back again. But when she told the Atlanteans of her decision, through thought communication, most of them didn't like it. This inability to understand the situation confirmed that the time was right to act.

Among those who were guided to places of safety were the ones known by legend as King Arthur and Merlin, as well as a woman not mentioned in the Arthurian saga called Avola. This was the origin of the name given to the area around Glastonbury in the west of England: Isle of Avalon. Arthur was a Son of the Godhead and Avola a Daughter of the Godhead. (I will explain what these terms mean a little later.) Merlin was Rakorski's lower self in a physical body; Magnu was also among this group. He had with him two 'very promising children' who, thousands of years later, are two of the people who channelled information for my first book, The Truth Vibrations. Many people would survive the coming changes and build the next civilization.

These people took with them everything that was needed from Atlantis, including certain crystals, and left for their places of safety. The Earth Spirit had planned very short bursts of physical change after which everyone would return to restore Atlantis and the Roof of Light. The land of Atlantis would be cleansed, but would not disappear completely.

All seemed well and under control, but, as Magnu put it, 'the biggest shock of our entire existence' was about to unfold. The being we call Lucifer was preparing to intervene in the most devastating fashion.

4.

The Fallen Angel

There has long been a 'devil' figure in human folklore and religion, and it comes with many names and in many guises. Most of these names refer to the same being, just as the various gods the different religions worship are, in fact, versions of the one Godhead.

Let us forget about evil. This does not exist. What does exist is imbalance, and when you are severely imbalanced, particularly in the negative direction, you can behave in very extreme and unpleasant ways. The name we have been given for the most imbalanced and destructive being in Creation is Lucifer, and this is the one who was to wreak havoc on this planet at the time of the end of Atlantis. I do not condemn him, for no one needs our love and understanding more than Lucifer in his present state of imbalance. He is a being who found himself on a downward spiral he was unable to stop.

Lucifer was created as a deva to work with the energy system. He would guide and support planet spirits, and when they disincarnated he would continue to do their work within the energy system at a minimum level until a new planet was formed. Devas have a particular ability to defuse much of the negative energy produced when a planet spirit disincarnates or goes through physical changes, and this is just as well or they would very quickly become imbalanced themselves. All that negative energy needs to be defused, because if it were to pass down the energy lines it would cause many problems for the whole system.

One of the reasons devas/angels are more immune than light beings are to negativity is that they do not have extreme emotions, unless they are in a physical body. When they are working on the light levels they have a deep compassion but do not allow emotions to affect them as light beings do. They have an ability to keep their minds focused on the wider view, and are able to see the positive reasons for the unpleasant scenes they observe, especially when a planet spirit disincarnates. This is a crucial element in a deva's make-up, and is a safeguard against the massive potential for emotional imbalance that such experiences can produce. This is how devas/angels manage to work so closely with the energy system without being severely imbalanced by the negative energies and experiences that come their way. Lucifer, however, was an exception. The Archangel Michael sent this communication:

Lucifer was a deva who worked with many others on the energy system of a very young planet called Ur, which means *divine*. This planet was beautiful and had great potential. It had a structure of minerals and crystals that are unknown to you, and surrounding it was a pink gas that radiated light from the planet outwards. Lucifer worked with the spirit of this planet, which had the task of using divine energy to act as a satellite power-source for some of the weaker and fairly new areas of that universe.

Lucifer had great respect and love for the spirit, probably more than is usually expected from a deva. Although we love you dearly, it is with an equal and unconditional love. It is balanced, because after all what is the point of adoring another? It only creates vanity and resentment. So Lucifer was slightly imbalanced towards positive energies. The point came when the spirit of Ur was no longer needed for that task, as the universe was evolving as it should, but a struggle arose because the spirit did not wish to leave, nor did Lucifer wish her to disincarnate. Although her physical body did eventually die, Lucifer carried a large amount of negativity as a result of the whole event. This negative experience should have balanced out his previous imbalance of positive energies, and then he would have been able to continue to work with the energy system and with other devas. But he never managed to regain his balance, and Creation's great learning experience was about to begin.

All this happened long before the Earth Spirit and Rakorski separated, but it was to be the start of a process that would severely affect both of them and, indeed, every being in Creation. The negative imbalance caused Lucifer to begin his fall down the frequencies and, because of the devas' built-in stability, no deva had fallen so far before. Lucifer decided to incarnate into a physical body in an effort to re-balance himself with a positive experience. In that life he worked on the energy system, but his life-plan was less than successful and his imbalance worsened. As time passed the imbalance became self-perpetuating as the negative energies now dominant within him attracted more negative experiences. Remember we are talking here of a period covering billions of years.

When this happens to light beings it is sad and disappointing for them, but eventually they find the right sequence of experiences to check their imbalance, and they begin their recovery from there. It is in no way a potential problem for Creation in general because, as light beings fall down the frequencies they 'forget' the details of how the energy system works. Every time you drop a frequency you have access to less knowledge, less wisdom, etc. So if light beings become severely imbalanced and prone to extreme behaviour they do not have the knowledge to disrupt the whole. With a deva it is different, and that is another reason why there is a need for them to be less open to emotional imbalance and negative energies.

A deva is created with the knowledge of the energy system already there, and they also have the ability to tap into the knowledge of all other devas. There is a constant flow of information and knowledge passing between them. This is necessary because they are working with energy lines and planets on all frequencies. So devas do not lose their knowledge when they move down the frequencies. Lucifer fell and fell until he reached the lowest frequency in Creation at that time – the one we are living on today. But while his imbalance to the negative extreme had slowed down his chakras and sent him tumbling through the frequencies, he was able to retain a detailed knowledge of the energy system. It was to be a telling combination. Michael said:

> Lucifer's fall down the frequencies was not sudden or swift, but quite gradual. He had many opportunities to regain his balance, and he brought many learning experiences to the Godhead and Creation, because a deva had not fallen down the frequencies because of imbalance before. Usually a deva only moves down to a lower frequency if it is to help a planet. If a planet is severely imbalanced it requires a great deal of knowledge and experience, but because all knowledge is shared equally among devas, whatever is known by the most knowledgeable ones who are working with a highly evolved spirit is also known by less experienced devas working with less evolved planet spirits and less complicated energy systems.

By now the Earth Spirit was within this planet and Rakorski was guiding her from the light levels. Lucifer was far away down the frequencies, and the light levels were constantly providing new opportunities for him to regain balance by helping with his life-plans for physical incarnations. But these physical lives were not successful. Lucifer's lower self was becoming more and more imbalanced, and these imbalances were constantly absorbed by the whole being at the end of each incarnation. The whole being we call Lucifer was dragged down by the inability of the lower self to keep to a karmic life-plan. The name given to this lower self is Satan, and his energies became the driving force within the whole being.

As the whole being Lucifer was falling he learned more about the negative side of Creation and the power of negative thoughts. Under the universal law of like-energy attracting like-energy Lucifer was attracting more and more negative energy to himself, and he would in turn be attracted to negative situations to absorb their energies, particularly when a planet spirit was disincarnating. He began to use these huge amounts of negativity destructively. He was on the bottom frequency, and the negativity created there began to seep upwards into the one above and so on. Gradually Lucifer was infecting the system, and when he realized his potential for harm and disruption he decided he could, and would, replace the Godhead. He was totally and utterly dominated by negative energies and by his lower self, Satan. Indeed he became so imbalanced he did not know he was imbalanced.

With his knowledge of the system he realized that if he could force the Earth Spirit to leave her planet and stop her sending out the harmonized and healing energies it would imbalance this universe and eventually all of Creation as more and more planets and beings fell into the sequence of self-perpetuating negative imbalance. This would be inevitable without the Earth Spirit's energies to help them stabilize themselves before their imbalance was out of control. Eventually this would bring all beings down to Lucifer's frequency, and the negativity that such a fantastic number of imbalanced beings would constantly create would seep up and up the frequencies until it reached the Godhead and sent him/her falling down to this frequency. Lucifer reckoned that his by now massive and unique experience of working with negative energies would mean that he would be able to take control once everyone was on his level.

But how could a being on the lowest frequency affect such a highly evolved planet spirit? Lucifer's plan was ingenious. As we have been told so many times in communications, the fallen angel may be misguided, but he is not stupid. He accumulated enough negative energy to imbalance a small planet called Lucifer, and ever since he has been known by that name. This is the planet we now call the Moon, and to avoid confusion I shall use that name from now on. The lower self, Satan, incarnated on the Moon and helped to create fantastic negativity. The imbalance was such that the Moon Spirit left, and Lucifer, now rejoined on the light levels by Satan, used all the power of his negative energies and those created at the moment the spirit left to direct the dying, spiritless planet towards another planet. The light levels had known that Lucifer was planning to use the Moon to create havoc, because his thought-forms were passed directly to the Archangel Michael through the devic information system and vice versa. Lucifer was thus aware of this and found a way to prevent the Godhead and Michael knowing exactly what he intended to do with the Moon. He formed a very large number of plans in his mind, but did not decide which one he would go for until the last possible moment, when he sent out the surge of negative energy that directed the dying Moon towards the Earth. The Archangel Michael said:

> There were a great number of possibilities, and we were in a waiting situation. Then Lucifer jumped into action. I was the deva guiding the Earth Spirit through the changes, and I along with many others was ready to work on the energies that needed to be harmonized during this period. I was in that role because it was vital, and so I was unable to react. I could do nothing but try to maintain some kind of harmony while the Earth turned over in front of my eyes. Lucifer had planned to remove me and the Earth Spirit in one action, but the Godhead, the Guiding Godhead and the Beyond helped me to stay, hold on to my frequency, and continue to harmonize while the Earth's physical body was in turmoil.

The physical bodies of the Earth and Moon did not collide, but their energy fields did. This happened at the precise moment the Earth was beginning what was planned to be the small axis shift at the end of Atlantis, and the effect was devastating. The Earth's stability was shattered. The Moon's original position was in the area that is known to astronomers as the Horse Head Nebula, and a new planet is now being formed at that point on the grid. As the Moon fell into this solar system all the planets were severely affected. The surface of the planets look bleak and lifeless because they are still recovering from these astonishing events. Rakorski said:

> What you see around you are the remnants of a devastated system, as many other planets were affected by the negative forces and the power of movement. The rings of Saturn and other debris in this solar system are the remains of other planets destroyed in the cataclysm. It was only the Roof of Light surrounding the Earth's gravitational and magnetic fields which slowed down the momentum, together with the power of the positive energies being directed by the Solar Logos towards and around the Earth. The Solar Logos was sending the very powerful healing Godhead energies that all planets receive during an axis shift.

> The power of these energies was enough to stop the Moon colliding with the Earth, but it became trapped within this planet's gravitational pull and began an orbit. At this time the force of the colliding energy fields and the power of the pull of gravity was enough to devastate the Earth. The same effect was seen throughout the solar system, resulting in varying degrees of damage.

The Earth's energy system was in tatters, and if it were not for the Archangel Michael somehow keeping open some of the energy arteries to the main network, the planet would not have survived. 'I owe him so much,' the Earth Spirit said, 'And his perseverance and positive attitude was wonderful for all of us.' Only about a thousand people on the planet survived, and even that was miraculous. Magnu described to us what happened on the surface:

> Land was torn in half. Life was snuffed out in an instant, and it was the start of what has become known as the cataclysm. There was water everywhere, tidal waves everywhere. Land froze within minutes.

Great mountains of rock were wrenched out of the Earth. Areas of land sunk – just collapsed and disappeared. There were violent eruptions, devastating landshifts, and the sea came in.

It was the biggest shock of our entire existence, and we were for the first time in thousands of lifetimes experiencing fear, an emotion we had forgotten about. We were scattered. The world had changed beyond recognition. Atlantis was no more. It took the Earth Spirit a very long time to speak again. She had been stunned and horrified by these events.

It was only because we were on such an extremely high frequency that the Earth or anyone survived. They certainly would not today. I was guided to a place not far from here (this information came through on the Isle of Wight, off England's south coast), and I remember the land shaking and shaking. I remember lying on the ground totally perplexed and wondering if I had not been guided after all.

I thought my physical life would end. We were all very afraid. This was not the axis shift that we had all known was coming. I was very anxious. What had happened to the Earth Spirit? I really thought that something had gone dreadfully wrong, and that the Earth Spirit had left the physical body of the Earth. What we were witnessing, I thought, was the collapse of the Earth as it began to disintegrate and die all around us.

Also we were suffering a sort of amnesia. We knew that things were not right, but our fear and anxiety had meant a fall down the frequencies. Who were we? Who had we been? What was happening? These questions went through my mind over and over again. We all still had many gifts, but as you know at times of fear or anxiety it is possible to block information. I waited for guidance, I waited for some answers. All around me was devastation and the departure from the physical to the light levels of all life forms. The Earth was not just shaking, it was leaping from its foundations.

Lucifer spoke to us from the Moon and told us of his plan to become the Godhead with or without us. We were very distressed and so confused.

The situation was this: There had been nearly 100 energy lines linking the physical level of the Earth with the grid network of Creation. Now there was just a handful, and the three main lines to the Godhead were no more. These links with the Godhead had been a specific target for Lucifer. All over the planet major energy sites had been severed from the energy lines linking them with the grid network of Creation. They were now open energy valves through which Lucifer could pour negativity and, they needed urgently to be shut down. The energy lines around the Earth itself were in tatters, and the Earth had fallen twelve frequencies immediately after the cataclysm.

The first response by Rakorski and the light levels was to regain control of the Moon. Vast amounts of positive energy were directed at that planet, and Lucifer had to leave as the vibrations quickened. A new planet spirit then incarnated and tried to save the Moon's dying physical body. She succeeded, and that courageous spirit is still there. When a steady orbit around the Earth had been established, Rakorski decided the Moon could help the Earth Spirit. Once the Moon had been re-linked to the grid, albeit in a limited way, a special energy line was created by the Godhead, Altimar and Rakorski between it and a mountain alongside what became the Inca site of Machu Picchu in Peru. This mountain has been given the name *Huayna Picchu* ('young peak'). It is to this place that large amounts of positive energy are sent to the Earth Spirit from the Godhead via the Moon, and this site replaced one of the three links with the Godhead which had been lost. Without this link there would be no Earth by now. Later they managed to create another line from the Solar Logos to Sun Island on Lake Titicaca in Bolivia.

Rakorski also needed to communicate with his lower self, existing in the physical body of Merlin. It was their joint efforts that made it possible to create a doorway to the astral level and receive information about what had happened and what was to be done. A doorway is different to the gateway I mentioned earlier, in that with a doorway you cannot return to your physical body afterwards, as Rakorski explained:

When Atlanteans wished to leave the physical they did not die as you know today. Many beings today die through illness or accident. Those that are fortunate die peacefully in sleep without pain. It was possible to create a doorway that left the physical body behind, like shedding a piece of clothing, or leaving your coat at the door. The doorway was created by crystals. Merlin had a crystal in his possession, but because the frequencies had fallen he needed our help to generate enough energy to create a doorway to the astral. He broke the crystal in half and created two posts of light. When placed at a certain point and with a certain energy, this created a powerful force, and using all his power and knowledge he created an energy field. I knew what he was doing and helped him as much as I could. Whenever the energy seemed to fade, Altimar and the Godhead brought it back. We helped Merlin because we needed to act immediately.

When Merlin returned from the meeting with those on the light levels he was no longer in a physical body. Instead he was a light body which manifested to look like Merlin and could appear and disappear. This, and his ability to do amazing things with the energies, led to the legend of Merlin the 'magician'. It was essential that Merlin left his physical body, because otherwise he would be affected by the falling frequencies around him and because information needed to be passed on very quickly and accurately. At times of such tremendous distress it is hard for people in physical incarnations to hear and receive guidance from the higher levels, and this information had to be got right.

Merlin and Arthur, who were father and son, had been guided to what is now Glastonbury in England for the duration of the changes, and they lived in the shelter of trees on what is now called Chalice Hill, although it had no name then. Merlin created his doorway just across from there, on the site of what became Glastonbury Tor. Shortly after the final cataclysm Merlin returned from his meeting. Arthur knew that Merlin would not return in a physical body, but he was less prepared for the nature of his message. Key energy sites around the British Isles were to be shut down to prevent them being used as open valves for Lucifer's negative energies.

While Rakorski and the light levels were removing Lucifer from the Moon, Arthur went off to gather together other Atlanteans who had been guided to Britain for the changes. It wasn't that Arthur was 'chosen' for this role or that he was the only one who could have done it. He was simply the only one who was there when Merlin returned with the news, it was Arthur or nobody. He found about twenty Atlanteans, most of whom are here again today. Some channelled information for *The Truth Vibrations*, and some are working in other ways. It was these former Atlanteans gathered together by Arthur who became known in the legends as the Knights of the Round Table.

While Arthur was getting this group together, Merlin manifested in what is now the Loch Ness area of Scotland. He visited another Atlantean, a woman called Avola. She possessed extraordinary gifts for one so young, and Merlin asked her to travel to Glastonbury to meet Arthur. She was not told why, but, like everyone Arthur was calling together, she had experienced the violent movement of the Earth and she wished to find out what was happening and what she could do.

The group met on Chalice Hill, and Merlin's spirit told them about the Moon, the condition of the Earth Spirit, his decision to go through the doorway, and how they had all fallen down the frequencies. There was sadness and confusion. Fear was in every heart, and the group was very divided about Merlin's request that they close the most powerful energy sites in the British Isles.

Many believed they could still fight back against Lucifer, and wanted to repair the system rather than close much of it down. But most areas of life had been wiped out, few beings remained on Earth in physical bodies, and the planet's surface was littered with the debris of the cataclysm. They were like innocent babes left in a wilderness, and somehow they had to pull themselves together.

They were persuaded to go ahead with the work. They discussed how they could prevent Lucifer from polluting the energy system most quickly and effectively, and they left feeling confident and determined. They named the hill where they met 'The Place of Truth,' and this has become confused with the legend of Camelot. Rakorski said:

> If Camelot is to represent truth and fellowship and that search for the higher self, then The Place of Truth is Camelot. People have since believed that the Holy Grail was a golden cup or chalice lifted at a time of fellowship, and it is easy to see how The Place of Truth became known as Chalice Hill.

Camelot, the Holy Grail and the Round Table are all symbolic of the need to work together, treat each other as equals, and seek the truth. Some have believed that Stonehenge was Camelot, but this was not the case. Stonehenge was a place where many of the surviving Atlanteans had come many times before the cataclysm to channel energies. It was built about 26,000 years ago by de-manifesting and re-manifesting stones from other parts of Britain, and was once the main energy site for the British Isles and part of Europe. It was not chosen as the meeting place after the cataclysm because the survivors wanted to protect it from the negative thoughts that were sure to be produced when Merlin revealed the dire situation at hand. It was eventually closed down as an energy site to stop Lucifer sending negative energies through it to the Earth Spirit. Avola created another site at nearby Avebury to replace it. Avebury was a much smaller version of Stonehenge, and was linked to what remained of the Earth's energy system. The stones at Stonehenge today are all that is left of a massive site, and they look very different since their lifeforce energies have been withdrawn. Many people still go there when the Sun rises at the start of the longest day of the year, although, of course, Stonehenge is no longer on its original alignment with the Sun because of the events described.

After their meeting at The Place of Truth Arthur and Avola travelled together, guided by Merlin, to close down energy sites and repair others where possible. It is the energy in the land at each site, each valve, which carries out the work required at that particular point in the system. If this energy is removed that work ceases to be done, and in this manner were the valves closed off. Once that energy was gone the site could no longer receive either positive or negative energies. Arthur, Avola and the others achieved this by working with highly evolved wood and crystal spirits, or by using their own bodies. All three methods could be used to absorb energies from a site. Members of the group could absorb the energy through their feet, and it would either stay within the energy pattern of their bodies until it could be moved to a new site, or it would be passed on through the chakras to the higher frequencies. The sites were not turned off like a switch, it could take a day or even a week for all the energy to be removed. It was exhausting and draining work and brought much sadness, because when a site was shut down they could feel the atmosphere fade into an uninviting flatness.

There was, however, no other way. The energy system was in shreds. Every area of land or water, every crystal, rock and mineral is in a certain place for a reason, yet now they had been scattered and hurled enormous distances. Many energy sites had been swallowed up, covered in water or torn apart. The network around the Earth was like a spider's web with large areas missing. Lucifer could complete his job of destroying the Earth if he could channel yet more negative energy through these open valves.

Let us put their task in context. There were no knights in

shining armour riding white horses across the countryside to dreaming castles with flags fluttering in the breeze, nor was there a sword called Excalibur. There were no swords. This was thousands of years before 'the days when knights were bold' and Excalibur is a symbol for the energies. Rakorski described what life was really like:

> There was very little sunlight. There were great clouds of dust and ash, and water and mist everywhere. It was cool and damp and very still. It was as if the whole world was in shock. In the distance you could hear the rumble of land moving and settling, the sound of rocks falling as land slipped down from precarious ledges. Trees were falling as their roots gave way, and there was an eerie silence broken only by the sounds of the Earth settling.

It was in these circumstances that the group made their way round the energy sites of Britain. When the task was complete they came together at The Place of Truth and Merlin appeared again to tell them the work was to be extended throughout the world. This was not well received. They had witnessed the effects of the falling frequencies and energy levels, and their own gifts of pyschic sight and hearing were fading. Their ability to communicate through thought-forms was also diminishing, and as the frequencies fell they were losing their knowledge and memories of Atlantis. They were desperately confused, and felt Merlin's plan was much too severe. Most of them still believed they should be repairing the energy system rather than closing down its most important sites.

They had free will to choose the path they wished to take. They could continue to close down the old sites and try to create new ones by travelling the world, or they could stay and work with the remaining energy sites in the British Isles. Of course they could have chosen to do neither, but Merlin emphasized that the Earth Spirit desperately needed positive energies to help her regain her balance and function as normally as possible. It was a time to stress working together rather than going out alone and trying to survive. It is indicative of how strongly they were affected by these events that one of the group, who is back on Earth today, still cannot let go of the deep resentment he/she felt 12,000 years ago when the gifts were being lost. It is affecting this person very deeply to this day. The group decided that while they would willingly continue to channel positive energies to the Earth Spirit, they would not close down any more sites. Arthur and Avola would have to do it alone, relying on help from individuals they met on their journeys and on Merlin's guidance.

I do not wish to portray Arthur and Avola as martyrs to the cause who went forward unquestioningly while others fell around them. They, too, were saddened by what they were doing, and there were many times when they questioned the wisdom of it all. It was a lifetime that brought distress and ill-treatment from those who opposed what they were doing, and there were occasions when they found it hard to understand what was happening. They carried on because they had a great love for the Earth Spirit. It was the infinite, unconditional love that the Atlanteans enjoyed, although it was becoming much harder to keep that alive as the frequencies fell. This love for all Creation made them very careful to prevent their doubts and confusions affecting their work. It kept them going initially, but this became very difficult as the Light reaching the planet was diminished and their tasks became harder.

They also communicated often with the Earth Spirit and, indeed, became her only source of information. The cataclysm had destroyed her direct communication channels with the Godhead and the light levels. Information could not be sent along the energy links that remained with Creation, because all their capacity was required for the energies necessary to secure her survival. Arthur and Avola were themselves confused and perplexed by the turn of events, and did not always portray events accurately when they communicated with the Earth Spirit. This was another reason why the energies needed to be turned down. If the Earth Spirit could not be guided she might decide to create more physical changes in an effort to restore her own system. This would have been fatal on the physical level, but with the power of her energies reduced she would find this very difficult.

Their task of turning down the energies was spread over many years. They were helped in their work by beings who came from other planets in what we would call spacecraft. It was not always possible for reasons I am not yet clear about, but Arthur and Avola were taken to many sites by spacecraft. Another of their key roles was to create new chakras that could receive and distribute energies. Every being, as I have outlined, has a series of energy points called chakras. That includes every planet and every large area of land on the surface, such as England. The heart chakra of each group of seven is the balance point. Imagine it as the centre of a pair of scales, with three chakras on one side and three on the other. The crown, third eye and throat chakras are the main links we have with the spiritual aspects of perceiving and receiving information from the light levels. The solar plexus, sacral and base chakras are concerned with the more physical aspects of our learning. In the centre is the heart chakra, which tries to balance the energies passing through the others, and if you can severely imbalance the heart chakra you can quickly imbalance the whole.

Now, because of the evolution which the Earth had reached before Lucifer intervened, her heart chakras had been very large sites, making them more difficult to defend against Lucifer. The potential for fatal damage to the Earth was great if he could affect these sites with all the negativity at his disposal. These heart chakras had to be either reduced in size so they were easier to defend with shields of positive energy or closed and new ones created.

The places where this could be done were several sites in Britain and one site in Denmark. If you closed down the 'valves' there it would turn down the heart chakra energy system for the planet. A combination was worked out in which certain sites were closed in a sequence that would be impossible for anyone to work out, even Lucifer. The early combination was comprised of Uffington in Wiltshire, Glastonbury, Avebury, Culloden in Scotland, the Isle of Wight, the place called The Moon Grove mentioned in *The Truth Vibrations*, and land near what is now Copenhagen. There were other sites, also. Rakorski summarized the situation:

These heart chakra energies that were either closed off or re-sited became known as the Green Dragon energies. The energies themselves vibrate to the same frequency as the colour green. It is a colour that exudes life, growth, balance, and calming of the mind and body. It is reliable and steady. Those that knew of the upheaval and loss of physical life, but failed to understand why it had happened, began to think of the Light as something terrible.

Gradually the Light was perceived as something powerful and awesome, and so fear began to creep into personal thoughts and behaviour. Over the many thousands of years between that time and now, the creation of the dragon myth has come about. In various cultures and stories dragons are seen as something to fear. The early Druids looked on the Earth Spirit as a dragon beneath the surface, because the story of the cataclysm had become so distorted that the events were seen as part of the Earth Spirit's desire for revenge. In the Bible the events are often portrayed as God's anger and revenge. In truth the cataclysm was really the mess left by Lucifer's designs on this planet.

When their work was nearly complete. Arthur searched for a place to find rest for a while and Avola decided to return to a small community of friends which had moved down from the Loch Ness area and settled south of Glastonbury. Also they both wanted to travel to the little communities all over the country to offer comfort and reassurance, tell people about the energy work,

and join them channelling energies. It was to be done at a much
slower pace than they had lived the previous few years, so they
could spend time with people, rest, and contemplate how they
were going to restore the energy system and take the Earth back
whence she came. Arthur went to what is now the Isle of Wight.
Today it is a small diamond-shaped island off the south coast of
England, but before the cataclysm it was much bigger and joined
the mainland. There was no English Channel until the cataclysm. Arthur went to a point near the village of Godshill,
which was to become part of a large network of energy lines. It
was here that Arthur turned the final key that closed down the
Green Dragon energies to the heart chakras.

At the same time Avola was due to channel at The Place of
Truth, and there were to be others positioned at points along the
line between her and Arthur. But shortly before this she was
killed, and her light body finished this part of the work. She had
been so affected by what had happened that she would probably
not have lived much longer anyway. Like Arthur she was weary
of trying to help others understand, and saddened by the lack of
fellowship, which increased with each fall down a frequency.
Arthur was also far weaker than he realized. When he knew that
Avola had returned to the light levels, and with Merlin now
rarely seen, he was downhearted. Rakorski decided to act:

> I called Avola and we agreed that Arthur's life and purpose on the
> physical seemed to be over. His higher self also felt it was time for
> him to leave, and so the spirit of Avola came to tell Arthur it was
> the moment to return to his home. Arthur left the physical, he
> closed his eyes and he was with us again. I was overjoyed to see him
> back on a level of light, which brought his suffering to an end.

During this period, as Arthur, Avola and Merlin were protecting
the system from Lucifer, they made a promise to the Earth Spirit
that they would return and put everything right. The Earth
Spirit remembers:

Merlin told me that the energy system was down to a minimum, but somehow they would find a way to restore the situation. He would work for this by receiving guidance from the Godhead and by guiding others in physical bodies. Merlin, Michael, Arthur and Avola promised me they would restore the system, if not in that lifetime then in a future one. They would do this with the same light workers, and until then they would work continually to gain greater experience and wisdom to make this possible.

With all those key sites closed down, Lucifer could no longer channel enough negativity into the Earth to destroy her. There were not enough sites still working for the Earth Spirit to absorb the amounts of negativity required to imbalance her to the extent that she would be forced to disincarnate. Had it stayed like that, the Earth would have settled down without falling many more frequencies, and the process of restoration could have begun.

But Lucifer, I repeat, is very clever. He had to find another way of making the Earth Spirit absorb large amounts of negativity, and find it he did. It was simple, but brilliant. Humanity would do it.

5.

Living in the Light

There is much to explain before it is possible to appreciate how Lucifer managed to use humanity to bombard the Earth Spirit with negative energy. It is necessary to understand the nature of a physical life on this or any other planet, and I will use this chapter to set out the background for what is to follow.

You will recall that we are created as a number of chakras joined together by a beam of Light energy, and that we then create for ourselves, by thought, a series of other energy fields called the spiritual, emotional, mental and etheric aspects. These aspects, together with the chakras and the beam of light, make up the whole light being – the real us. Here is a summary of what these aspects are designed to do on both the physical and light levels.

The Spiritual Aspect

This is our link with divine guidance from the Godhead, the Guiding Godhead and the Beyond. It receives the messages they send along the energy system, and passes back into the system all that our light being learns with each new experience. If we can stay in touch with this aspect of our being it will be easier to focus on the wider perspective of life and Creation. It also makes use of our crown, third-eye and throat chakras, and tries to keep us in touch with the light levels.

The Emotional Aspect

This helps us to learn from our emotions and keep them under control. If we are the subject of another's intolerance or anger, the emotional aspect will work hard to help us understand the reasons for that experience and what we can learn from it. The emotional aspect can also trigger certain emotions to give us the opportunity to learn from them. On this low frequency our emotions tend to be imbalanced and extreme, and the emotional aspect is working flat out most of the time to give us some sort of emotional stability. The emotional aspect makes use of our solar plexus, sacral and base chakras during our physical life. This is why we feel our emotions as a sort of ache in the solar plexus area.

The Mental Aspect

This offers us logic, reason, and, if we use it well, wisdom. It helps us when we are in a physical body to be rational, ask the right questions, follow guidance, and make good choices. It needs to be balanced with both the emotional and spiritual aspects. This is to avoid, on the one hand, being cool, detached and unaffected by what we see and experience, and on the other, being weighed down by emotional turmoil. No aspect can work in isolation, they have to work with and balance one another. The mental aspect provides balance and therefore works through the heart chakra as it searches for clarity, creativity, enlightenment and love of the self.

The Etheric Aspect

This is the organizer, and any problems will show themselves here first before manifesting as a physical or mental illness. On the light levels it gathers all the necessary information together that we require for a physical incarnation, while on the physical level it organizes the electrical system of the body – the messages sent out by the brain and down the spinal cord to every area. All aspects interact constantly and if one is having difficulties it can affect the others. This is how our emotions can cause physical illness. If the emotional aspect disrupts the etheric, this will, in turn, disrupt the organization of the physical body. Students of acupuncture have long been aware of this connection: acupuncture aims to keep the energies of a being in harmony, so maintaining health at the physical level. The etheric aspect has another crucial role, which I will come to in a moment.

Each aspect makes a contribution to the debate that takes place on the light levels as to which experiences would be most beneficial for the whole light being in its journey towards balance, wisdom, and higher frequencies. Once agreement is reached, a life-plan is put together for the next physical incarnation, which will produce those experiences. It may be that a being needs a positive experience to balance a negative one, or have done to him or her what he or she has done to others. Remember the light being uses free will to decide the course it wishes its physical lives to take. It is its decision and its alone. Endless guidance is available from the higher levels if requested, but there is never any compulsion. Nor, I should emphasize, does all this mean that everything we do in a physical life is pre-ordained before we arrive. We are always subject to the free will of ourselves and of others, and of course this can radically affect our life-plan once we are in a physical body.

An individual life-plan will involve many other beings, and together they will work out a series of situations they wish to experience with each other. This is for karmic reasons, to balance their previous experiences together and to arrange situations that all wish to go through for their personal development. Everyone helps everyone else to produce the life-plans they need, to the benefit of all. Rakorski said:

> This system of reincarnation sets up a complicated network of relationships linked by karma and a need to experience karma as a result of attitudes from a previous life. We come across many thousands of beings in one incarnation. Multiply this over many lifetimes and it is easy to see how we can be linked with beings in many universes over thousands and thousands of years. This is why guidance and planetary influences are available, to help beings stay on their karmic course and remove those links.

> Karma is a way of life. The words 'law' or 'principle' are used only to give you some idea of the fundamental or basic structure of Creation. It is the way evolution throughout Creation is constructed. It is foolish to think that these laws are made to be broken. We don't stand over you with a big stick saying 'think of the karmic consequences of this or that action.' However, it needs to be understood that it is there and woven into all life-plans. But, of course, as a being constructs his or her life-plan it is possible to see learning and evolution from a much greater perspective. There is vision and creativity on the light levels that is currently absent from the Earth. In fact we empathize with those on this low frequency and understand the frustration that is created from uninspired and negative behaviour.

We may come to a planet to work for the Light, to bring the truth or work on the energy system, or both. But even then we will also have a life-plan aimed at giving us the necessary experiences and the opportunity to break karmic links with other beings. When we act in an imbalanced way towards another, we build up karmic 'debts', the same is true of those who act in an imbalanced way towards us. We will need to incarnate with them again and try to balance everything out between ourselves by acting in a different way in a similar situation. Until that is done it will not be possible to progress to the next frequency.

It is an obvious sign of imbalance if someone believes that a person's colour, creed, religion or race makes them inferior. A feeling of superiority or inferiority is the manifestation of imbalance. It follows that those who have condemned and abused others on these grounds will need to reincarnate as a person of that very colour, creed, religion or race, to experience what they have made others experience. If only humanity realized this truth, what anger, hatred and suffering could be avoided.

You can see there are many karmic patterns that are weaved into life-plans before we enter a physical body. There is karma to balance out between individuals and experiences to be arranged between beings to their mutual evolutionary benefit. If we keep to our life-plans, the people around us, parents, children, friends, work-mates, are not there by accident but by design. Karma operates on every level, from people to organizations, countries, and planets, and on each level the same truth applies: What we do to others we are really doing to ourselves. Karma is not a punishment, but a means of finding balance, and it offers us very pleasant experiences as well as the less pleasant ones. There is positive karma and negative karma. Everyone on the planet at this time has karma with the Earth Spirit because of past actions, and they have returned to take this unique opportunity to balance out that karma. This is why the population of the world is so great at this time.

Akashic Records

Everything we do in any lifetime on the physical or light levels is imprinted on an energy known as the Akashic records. This is our personal 'copy' of our entire existence, and through this our current karmic situation is always available to us. Some New Age writers refer to these records as the Halls of Learning. It is not actually a hall or building, but an energy which we can tune into and gather information from. Rakorski said:

> The energy of karma from the Akashic records is always carried within a being. If he or she has in a previous life created great negative karmic links with another it is possible to cancel that and find balance either by repaying the debt directly to the other being or by repaying it to another. If he or she was incredibly hostile to his neighbours and went out of his way to make their lives unpleasant so that they suffered spiritually, emotionally, mentally and physically, then he or she would have built strong negative karmic links on a very personal basis. Those events would be imprinted on the Akashic records of both the individual and his or her neighbours. However, in a later life this being may be highly inspired to serve another. Now there would be a choice: either to accept a positive karmic link on a personal basis or take the opportunity to cancel out the negative karma against the neighbours. Because everyone is able to see the wider picture on the light levels they can make the appropriate choice. It may even be one of repeating this several times to ensure that the lesson is well and truly learned.

Often when we behave out of character it can be the higher self setting up a karmic situation and guiding us into it. Once there we are left to decide how to react, and this gives us the opportunity to use our free will to act in a way that will balance out a previous experience. If we choose not to react in that way we can build up more karma for ourselves. Unless these karmic situations are successfully met we continue to carry that karma, and this holds back our progress and evolution. So you can see that here is another example of why we should not judge others for their actions. We don't know the details of other people's life-plans, and what appears to us to be unacceptable behaviour could well be an essential part of their personal development which has been arranged and agreed to by all parties involved before they incarnated.

The principles of karma can mean that we can deny people experiences they wish to have because we want to protect them. Shielding others from some experiences may be our understandable reaction on the physical level, but they will not thank us when we return to the light levels. As Rakorski said in *The Truth Vibrations*: 'True love does not always give the receiver what it would like to receive, but it will always give that which is best for it.' If we listen to our guidance we will know when to step in to protect someone and when simply to give him or her our love and support and allow them to go through a karmic experience.

When the time arrives to incarnate, the light being creates by thought a duplicate set of chakras to match its own, and adds to them a certain amount of personal energy along with the Akashic record and certain other energy packages. It is this combination that enters the physical body. As you know, we call this combination the lower self, and the rest of the whole being, which stays on the light levels, the higher self. Their two roles are clearly defined: the lower self is the one that experiences in a physical body, and the higher self provides guidance from the light levels. Both have free will. The higher self has the free will to guide and the lower self has free will to accept or ignore that guidance as it sees fit.

How much of a whole being's personal energy incarnates will depend on past experiences in a physical body. If we have a history of allowing the physical body to dominate us, a much smaller proportion will incarnate because of the potential for imbalance. If we have a record of working well on the physical, a larger proportion of our energy will incarnate, and in these circumstances other beings will help the higher self to guide the lower self during that lifetime. If an incarnation is progressing well it is possible for the whole being to pass on more of their energies, and this can have a considerable effect on the behaviour and understanding of the lower self.

We also bring with us the information we need to follow our chosen life-plan. It may be that we will wish to experience a life in music or sport. To make this possible, the etheric body gathers together 'experience packages' available on the light levels which we bring with us to the physical body. When the time is right and if we follow the life-plan, these packages of experience can be activated and give us the knowledge and skills we require. When we hear of child prodigies and 'born athletes, musicians' or the like, we are seeing the effect of these packages being activated and used by that particular person. Every time someone has an experience of any kind, the learning is available for all of us to tap into and use in these experience packages.

Exactly when we enter the physical body depends entirely on what we wish to experience. Some will enter with the sperm, others will wait until the moment of birth. We all arrive ready and willing to follow the life-plan agreed beforehand, and the time we are born is also no accident. We are trying to ensure that our arrival coincides with a planetary sequence that makes available to us the best possible energies that can help us with our life-plan. The energies around us when we are born can have a significant impact on how we will behave in a physical life.

It would be of no value if we knew beforehand everything we had come to experience and why. If that were so we could just go through the motions of reacting to situations in the way we hoped we would. How could we learn in these circumstances? To overcome this we 'forget' such information when we enter a physical body, although we carry deep within us all the knowledge necessary to cope with the challenges we have set up for ourselves. Our link with the life-plan is our higher self, who knows precisely what the lower self has come to experience and with whom. There are energy channels which link the chakras and the mental, emotional, spiritual and etheric aspects of the higher self to the lower self in the physical body. It is through these channels that the various aspects try to help and support us on the physical level in the ways I have described. Rakorski expanded on this:

> We have all experienced this help. Some people seem to be in the right place at the right time, some have a 'gut' reaction, intuition, or premonition. Your body also carries all the information that you need for a successful life-plan. Guidance, planetary influences, support from other physical beings – these are all bonuses. You as individuals actually carry all the answers to any problems or experiences that you encounter on the physical. So, you may ask, 'Why am I not more successful?' Well, first we need to define the word 'successful'. If you live life to the full, not just existing but using your experiences – positive and negative – to help yourself understand, give and share, grow and develop, then although life may have been tough you will have completed a successful life-plan.

> Success to us is not measured by financial or social status. Success for an individual is finding a balance of negative and positive energies, gaining knowledge, breaking karmic links, and covering new ground for even greater learning. When an individual achieves this we rejoice. Every individual can find out what has happened in the past and what needs to happen now for the journey to continue. To find this information it is necessary to find peace on the physical level. Quiet meditation helps beings reveal to themselves who they really are. It means opening the eyes and carefully peeling back the protective layers that we surround ourselves with, and looking at the real being. It is tough, but extremely rewarding.

The higher selves of all of us are working together on the light levels to lead us into the correct situations. As Rakorski said, we feel this guidance as intuition, a feeling of being drawn to certain people and places. Often we talk of these moments as 'coincidence' and we say 'well, fancy meeting you here, what a small world.' If we follow this intuition or gut feeling we are following the guidance from our higher selves, who are sending us thought-forms and other energies to keep our life-plan on course. On the high frequencies this planet once enjoyed it was comparatively easy to be guided in this way. The beings were much more evolved and the link with their higher selves was strong. They knew how the system worked, and listened to these messages of guidance. On the highest sub-planes of the Atlantis frequency, of course, you could walk through a gateway to the Astral Plane and have a conversation directly with your higher self to discuss how your life-plan was going.

Clearly we do not have the luxury of a gateway today. As the planet has fallen down the frequencies so it has become increasingly difficult to maintain this open link with our higher selves and other guidance. Our physical bodies have become less finely tuned, and our knowledge of the existence of this system of guidance has faded and in many cases disappeared on the physical level. The potential for losing touch with our guidance, and so our life-plans, has grown with every decade since Atlantis, and is now enormous. The life-plan can be severely affected if we lose touch with our guidance, or if others who agreed to be with us lose touch with theirs. We may not even be born if those who agreed to be our parents cannot hear their guidance and choose not to have children. Higher selves are constantly communicating with each other on the light levels to rearrange personnel and situations to ensure that at least part of the life-plan is achieved. The ultimate option for a lower self if they do not wish to continue with a physical life is to commit suicide, but when this happens the karma they are avoiding will still need to be faced in the future if they wish to progress.

When someone has reached a time when major choices have to be made about whether to continue with the life-plan or go in another direction he or she can be seriously affected. To the person involved it will simply be a choice between two courses of action, but in reality it will be a choice between life-plan or no life-plan, and the inner light being will know this. Such times of decision can play havoc with the energies both within and without. It can create a force of complicated energies, and if these are not handled well it can have a devastating effect on the person. This is when the need for guidance from the light levels can be so helpful, to help us make the right decisions and find balance.

The higher self also helps us during a physical incarnation by sending us certain energies known as the Rays. These are energies designed to have specific effects on our thinking and attitudes, should we wish to use them. It has been believed that there are seven such rays, but there are an infinite number as Creation expands. At the moment most people on the physical level of this frequency work with a maximum of seven, while on the light level of the frequency we can work with up to thirteen. These rays are designed to help all life-forms to speed their understanding, wisdom, and thus their evolution. The rays work through the chakras, and this is why we have seven chakras on the physical level of this frequency and up to thirteen on the light level. Each of the rays is on the same frequency as a colour, and if we wear that colour we can absorb and generate that ray more efficiently. They are:

Ray One (Violet)

This helps us to see the wider picture, to rise above the immediate here and now. It is a ray that encourages greater vision and helps us to act accordingly. We move away from interpreting events on the basic physical level and towards seeing the truth with a higher level of understanding, a more spiritual understanding.

Ray Two (Turquoise)

This is the *Ray of Love and Wisdom*, and it can help us all achieve these qualities. This is a ray that most beings on Earth today have come to work with and tune in to. But negativity is denying so many the full potential of this wonderful energy. Royal blue carried the energy of spiritual love and yellow the energy of wisdom; together they form this ray.

Ray Three (Red)

This is known as the *Ray of Intelligence*, but the word is used in its widest sense. This is not merely about brain power, how many facts you can remember, or whether you can recall the formula of complicated equations. Intelligence is opening the mind to information that is less than obvious. A scientist can tell you about the speed of light between planets and the distance between planets and stars, but we are limited in intelligence if we can see only that which can be proved.

Ray Four (Green)

This ray is widely known in the New Age movement as *Harmony Through Conflict*. It does not simply mean learning to live in harmony by having first to go through some catastrophe. It can also mean learning to curb your temper and anger by seeing the unpleasant consequences for yourself and others. It helps us to use a negative situation to change our thinking so that we begin to act positively.

Ray Five (Silver)

This is known as *Concrete Mind and Science*. It is sent to all planets whatever their stage of evolution. This will be a very useful ray to help humanity learn to use, and respect, the resources of the Earth. The Atlanteans and others had such knowledge and respect. They used the energies of crystals and water, and understood the relationship between one life-form and another. This philosophy can be summarized thus: Take only what you need, and no more.

Ray Six (Pink)

This is the *Self-awareness Ray* known also as love and devotion. It is a ray that carries information about the healing of the body and spirit, and its power will increase towards the end of the geological changes that are to come. After the axis shift people will need to be as pure as possible as they rise up the frequencies with the Earth Spirit. Ray Six will help them understand how to heal themselves from within, and they can then take this knowledge to others.

Ray Seven (Gold)

This comes via the Sun. The New Age name for this ray is *Law and Order and Ceremonial Magic*. It is known to us as the *Rakorski Ray*, because he is responsible for how this ray is used in his role as Lord of all Civilization. He said:

> There is no magic of the hocus-pocus variety. Magic here refers to the wonders of Creation, and when you are on a certain frequency you can make things happen with this ray. It helps you appreciate the potential of the energies and how to work with them to your and their full potential. Neither is Law and Order the same as you understand it today. It is karma, free will, reincarnation, acceptance, responsibility, love, the basic bottom-line thinking behind Creation. No matter where you are these same principles apply, and this ray helps us appreciate and use them to speed our evolution.

Rays Eight to Twelve

These rays do not apply to us on the physical level of this frequency. They ceased to reach the Earth in large quantities about 3,000 years ago when we dropped to a frequency that no longer carried the information and wisdom that allowed people to use them. We will be able to use these rays again as we rise back up the frequencies after the changes. The Earth Spirit receives them, however: they are sent to her to help maintain her balance at times of extreme imbalance, and are absorbed by the rocks, crystals and minerals.

Ray Thirteen (Pure White)

This is known in this universe as the *Christ Ray*. This is an energy that Jesus channelled, and this is the origin of his title Jesus 'Christ'. The Christ is not a person, but the energy Jesus could channel. The nature of this ray is beyond our comprehension on this frequency, but basically it is an energy that carries information that will bring wisdom and a new way of life. It brings an understanding of the wisdom of the truth and how to use that understanding. It is the ray that, more than any other, will transform the world. The Christ Ray only comes at a time of change, and it is returning to the Earth now for the first time in 2,000 years.

As the rays pass down the frequencies the Godhead and beings such as the Solar Logos, Rakorski and many others add their own energies in response to the changing needs of the planets, stars and life-forms under their guidance. The rays are in the environment around us; they come to the planet along the energy grid or via other planets and star systems, and sometimes are channelled in by certain people when a time of transformation is at hand.

Special combinations of the seven rays are also passed directly to us by our higher selves. This combination of rays will be designed to match our life-plans and will complement the energies of those planets that most influence us because of the time of our birth. Most people on Earth today will have rays two, three, four or five as part of their personal combination, because of the desperate need for all of these at this time. If, however, people become de-linked from their higher selves, this personal combination of rays can no longer help them. They will then only have access to the rays available in the environment – these will necessarily be weaker and affected by all the surrounding negativity and imbalance, but at least even de-linked beings are not left without any support or access to the rays. Their main planetary influences will also be there to help them keep to their life-plan.

There you have the background to a physical incarnation, and you may be able to see already how Lucifer planned to exploit it. He needed to use humanity to produce negativity through negative thought. But to imbalance a planet spirit enough to force her to disincarnate would take immense amounts of negativity, an impossible task as long as the truths of reincarnation, karma and the energy system were known and accepted. Destroying the truth about Creation in the human mind was fundamental to his plan. To do that, and to bring about the circumstances in which humans would think negatively and act negatively towards others, he needed to de-link the lower self from the higher self during a physical life. On the light levels beings know of Lucifer's ambitions and design their life-plans overall to produce positive, not negative, energy.

Once we are in the physical body Lucifer and other negative forces go to work on us, although if we remain balanced he cannot affect us. They are looking for weaknesses to exploit, and once they have found them they can make them more severe by sending us negative energies and thought-forms. Once this happens our links with our higher selves and all our aspects begin to weaken steadily. Negative energies operate particularly through the emotions, making us angry, fearful, stressful, resentful, greedy, envious, and as confused as possible. This can make us lose touch with the guidance of the emotional aspect, which is trying to help us understand the consequences of our imbalanced emotions. Lucifer does not do this by working on everyone individually, he seeks rather to affect most people by generating and directing negative energies into the environment along with a constant stream of thought-forms. If people are imbalanced they can find themselves tuning in to these energies and thoughts, and behaving accordingly.

Lucifer both stimulates extreme emotions and cuts us off from the guidance that would help us control them. If we lose the guidance of the mental aspect we lose the ability to think rationally and keep a clear head, so we are much more easily confused and led astray. He works extremely hard on those in power. He encourages them to lead economics, politics and science in the direction he wants and he seeks to cause conflict on every level from personal argument to world war. He also picks out any highly evolved beings who come to this planet because he knows if they can be made to think negatively their thought-power will produce large amounts of negative energy.

Once such thought patterns and emotions are established the messages of guidance from the higher self can no longer get through as they should. Children are often very open psychically, and see and hear many things their elders do not. This is because we are born to be psychic and have good links with the light levels. But once a child has been told not to be silly when he or she recounts a psychic experience that child is affected emotionally and the channel is closed down. Some children have a very powerful ability to see and hear other frequencies, and their gifts may be diminished by the reaction of others but not necessarily lost forever. They may choose to keep this ability hidden as their little secret, and only later in life allow it to come forward.

Most people close down their channels of guidance once they

have been on Earth long enough to become affected by their weaknesses and imbalance – and then, as a consequence, by Lucifer. Once we are de-linked from our guidance we become like a boat without a paddle or rudder, drifting aimlessly and easy prey for Lucifer and other negative forces to manipulate. They become our guide. This can develop into a self-perpetuating process, with negative imbalance encouraging people to think negatively, so increasing the negative imbalance, which encourages people to think even more negatively, etc., etc. This is how Lucifer planned to destroy the world, and for 12,000 years it has worked brilliantly, although it is only over the last 100 years that this process has become the runaway roller coaster it now is.

Let me make one thing crystal clear, however. Although we may be subject to these extreme negative forces, we do not have to succumb to them. Not everyone has done so by any means. Witness all the people doing selfless and magnificent work around the world today. If we do not wish to be guided by Lucifer we do not have to be. We can ask for guidance from the light levels, tune in to the Light, and seek that inner knowledge and guidance we all possess. We can refuse to allow our emotions to dominate us, and can search for that ability to love and accept all people whoever they are and whatever they do. When we have this outlook on life Lucifer can no longer pull our strings, and we automatically tune in to the Light, the rays and all the other energies we need. We have a responsibility to do this for ourselves, the Earth, and all Creation. Lucifer may be powerful and clever, but he should not be used as an excuse for all negative behaviour. We make the choices about how we react and behave, and so the responsibility is ours, not Lucifer's.

There is something else to appreciate about a physical incarnation. I know it sounds incredible, but it is true. Everything that happens on this physical level has already happened on another level, called the *Etheric*. There is a need to make a record of everything that ever happens in Creation. These are the records that our etheric aspects scan when they are putting together the experience packages we all bring to a physical incarnation. It is a permanent record of every being's experience that is there for us to learn from and use without necessarily having to go through that exact experience ourselves. It is a sort of infinite library of experience. Every time beings act, whether we like what they are doing or not, they are adding to the library of experiences to which we all have access. No experience is wasted either by the individual concerned or by Creation. This record cannot be made from physical energies, it must be made with non-physical or spirit energies on the light levels, and the area where this happens is known as the Etheric. We also have that permanent individual record of our experiences called the Akashic record, but that is not the same. The Etheric is the record of everything that has ever happened in all Creation.

Think of the Etheric as a gigantic videotape that includes the past, present and future of all Creation. The Etheric level is a mirror-image of Creation, and is made from a unique kind of energy. It is important to remind ourselves that the various levels and frequencies are not piled on top of each other. They share the same space, and every object and life-form has within an etheric aspect. If you look at a cup you see only the physical part of the cup. In fact in the same space occupied by the physical cup is its etheric double, made of non-physical energy. Some psychics can see this energy and I have begun to do so myself. The etheric looks like a photographic negative of the physical. This double exists on the frequency of the etheric level and because all things have such a double, the etheric level is a mirror image of Creation made of this non-physical energy. It must always be so for one simple reason. If an object or being does not have an etheric double it cannot exist, because everything happens and is created on the etheric before it appears on the physical.

Predictions come in two forms. There are predictions that foretell (usually well in advance) what is going to happen, and predictions that describe what has already happened on the etheric level. The former are subject to revision because of free will and changing circumstances, but the latter will definitely happen because the etheric recording has been made. It is, incidentally, by working on the etheric level in co-operation with the rock, mineral, crystal, land and water spirits that the Earth Spirit can ensure that everything ends up in the right place during physical changes. Every building, object, blade of grass and level of existence is duplicated on the etheric. London on the etheric is in exactly the same place as London on the physical, but it is made of a non-physical energy. Humans, animals, higher and lower selves and all life-forms have etheric aspects, also. This is the part of our being that makes the 'recording'.

This is how it works. The etheric aspect of the lower self goes off to record situations. It remains linked to the physical body by an umbilical cord of energy through which messages pass from the physical brain. The brain, therefore, is playing its part in the way the etheric aspect behaves during the recording procedure. How it behaves is entirely down to either the free will of the higher self (if the being is linked and listening to guidance) or the lower self (if those links are weak) – or sometimes to a mixture of both the higher and lower self. A great deal can be recorded in one session, because things happen much more quickly on the etheric, and the higher you go up the frequencies the quicker they happen. So your etheric aspect has read this book before, only much more quickly than you are doing now! Most of the time we are not aware that this is going on, because it occurs on the subconscious level of our brain, which is sending the messages during the recording. Sometimes, however, we can be affected by the process. You know those occasions when you 'lose' time? You may be driving along, and suddenly wonder where the last few miles have gone, or you forget where you put things you were holding, or what you'd just been doing. These are times when an etheric recording is being made and your sub-conscious is working so hard it affects your conscious mind.

Remember that the etheric aspect governs the physical body, so in the simplest of terms the etheric aspects of everyone and everything are programmed during these recordings to make the physical body behave subsequently in exactly the same way. When the higher and lower selves are working as one it is so much easier for the higher self to arrange these etheric recordings so that they set up the karmic situations that are part of one's life-plan. It is also possible for the higher self to hold back certain recordings until it believes the time is exactly right to bring them to the physical. I have asked on several occasions how all these etheric recordings can be brought to the physical at different times. You would think it would be chaos and a nightmare to organize. The reply is always that many things are possible on the light levels that we find hard to comprehend here.

De-linked lower selves do not get the opportunity to work out karma because of the difficulty in organizing, and guiding them to, the necessary situations with the necessary people. Far from working out karma these beings can spend their entire physical life building up more and more karma. Over a number of physical lives they can become swamped by negative karma, and the further down the frequencies the whole being will fall. This is what Lucifer wants and works so hard for. He cannot do this by changing or tinkering with the etheric recordings. He can only affect them by affecting the way people behave as the recordings are taking place. Let us look in more detail at how this is done. The messages of guidance come down the energy channels from the higher self and from all the various aspects, and travel through the chakras to the physical brain. The brain then distributes this information to the lower self and, during an etheric recording, this is then passed along the umbilical cord of energy to the etheric aspect. In a fully linked being the etheric aspect thus has guidance from all levels of higher and lower self as it decides how to behave during the recording. The more the lower self is de-linked, the less information and guidance it receives at these times, and the potential for negative behaviour is increased accordingly. A lower self is never totally de-linked, but the messages can become so weak and distorted that the effect is the same.

In these circumstances the only information and guidance the etheric aspect is receiving during the recording comes from the physical brain and the lower self. In turn, the only information the brain is receiving comes from whatever it has seen or heard through the eyes and ears. The etheric aspect is receiving its guidance on these occasions only from the brain, the seven chakras and beam of Light within the physical body, and these are being guided only by what is happening in the physical world around them. Add to that the negative thought-forms being directed at them by Lucifer, and is it any wonder that people de-linked in this way laugh, scoff and condemn when they are presented with the truth about Creation? How can they be expected to understand these things when they are only receiving their information and 'guidance' from this physical level? It is such fundamentally de-linked beings that start World Wars and behave in a horrific or extreme manner. Given the current state of affairs on this frequency it is astonishing that so many people still remain linked and live wonderful lives of love and compassion.

The de-linking from the higher self can have serious consequences for the health of the physical body. The cells of the brain are coated with a divine energy to help the brain stay in touch with the channels of guidance, but if the brain becomes de-linked these cells can go into shock. They panic when they become aware of losing contact with guidance, because on such a low and unwelcoming frequency this can be very traumatic. Such brain cells affect the other cells of the body and there are many ways this can manifest itself in illness and disease.

The human body is an incredible gift from the Godhead. It deserves to be treated with reverence, respect and love, both by the individual and all other beings. The design for the first physical bodies on Earth was created by the Godhead, and the body has changed and adapted itself as it has risen up and fallen down the frequencies. Since Atlantis it has changed from taking in energy externally to digesting energy from food internally. The light levels have had to step in to help here and there, but generally this process has been achieved by the body itself. The body can also inherit defects caused by the diseases or emotional experiences suffered by those who incarnated into physical bodies earlier in the same ancestral or 'blood' line. These defects are passed on in the genes from generation to generation. The body evolves and adapts independently of light beings. Their evolutions are separate; one is the life-form and the other is the shell used for experience and learning. When light beings are putting together a life-plan they take into account these ancestral lines and the various inherited defects because of the different opportunities for experience they present.

Like the Earth, our physical bodies have 'ley lines' carrying energy to all areas. The human version are called *meridians*. They give the physical body information, help heal, repair and rebuild, and can also help a physical being operate in harmony with his or her emotional, mental and spiritual levels. The meridians can carry energies sent to this level by far and distant planets that can help us fulfil a life-plan. When many energy lines are not working and minimal energy is getting through this can manifest as cancer, leukemia, and many other diseases. Cells are either rebuilding with extreme negative energy and are therefore 'eating' the balanced cells or their immunity is destroyed and diseases can get through the defences.

The brain and the physical body have enormous potential to receive and transmit energies, but only a fraction of this potential is used on this low level. Indeed the body is barely functioning on this frequency and because of this it develops weaknesses. It becomes vulnerable to all kinds of negative vibrations such as those in food preservatives and colourings. Anything that is not organic is harmful to the body in its current condition and even organic food can be affected by pollution and negativity. These affects on the physical body create yet more negative energies because of the suffering they bring and can make it more likely for that person to be de-linked. It is a vicious circle that only love can break.

So there you have the basic elements of a physical incarnation, the nature of the physical body and the way Lucifer has manipulated this system in an attempt to control our behaviour. It is a lot to take in all at one go, but these are the points to remember: We come with a life-plan that offers the experiences we feel we require to speed our evolution; we build up karma with other beings, pleasant and less pleasant, which needs to be balanced out by experiencing what we have made others experience or by reliving the same situation again and acting in a different way; what happens on the physical level has already happened on the etheric; and if we lose touch with the guidance of the higher self and inner self we can become easy victims for Lucifer and other negative forces.

Now we have set out the essential background to Lucifer's plan, we can continue our story of the Earth and humanity and why we are all where we are today.

6.

The Great Divide

It took 3,000 years for the Earth to calm down after the cataclysm, and it was only 9,000 years ago that people began to organize themselves into communities and find ways of using the remaining energies to survive.

With the energy system at only minimum levels they could no longer live purely on the energies in the water and environment. They had to supplement these by consuming the energies contained in plant life. This is why we need to eat food now – to make up for the low energy levels in the world around us. As the frequencies continue to rise in the years ahead we will have no need to do so.

The communities which emerged as the Earth settled were those of the so-called 'primitive cavemen'. They were anything but primitive, and indeed were on a higher frequency than we are at present. They did not go around with giant stone clubs saying 'Ug'. They knew of the energy system and what had happened, and they channelled positive energies to the Earth Spirit. They also had many nomadic communities which travelled between energy sites. A spoken language did begin to develop as the frequencies fell and it became more difficult to communicate through telepathy. Instead thought energy was slowly turned into sound energy for communication, but it was a little more sophisticated than 'Ug'! These people farmed the grasslands, taking from the land only what they needed, and realized what riches were available in the plant kingdom. They were, I suppose, the first homoeopaths.

In this period, as the Earth began to calm down, Lucifer was contacted directly by the Godhead. The light levels had no wish to see the deva cause any more devastation or create any more karma for himself. The Godhead would help him to plan his incarnations, and his karmic journey back to balance could begin. It would be long and tough, because the negative karma he'd built up with so many planets and life-forms was enormous, but Lucifer, the whole being, decided at this stage to give it a try. The Godhead had made it clear that the karma would need to be faced eventually. What was to be gained by building up yet more? If Lucifer had been successful with his incarnations then all his plans to use human thought to destroy the Earth would have been forgotten as he became more balanced. The idea was for the lower self, Satan, to start by incarnating and to work with a man called Aktaurus as they helped to restore the energy system. In this way Lucifer, through Satan, could begin to repay karmic debts.

Aktaurus was what has become known on Earth as a Son of Man. These are beings who come with a gift for channelling the very powerful energies needed by the Earth and all life-forms, and for repairing the energy system of the planet. All planets are visited by such beings when necessary. The female version is called a Daughter of the Earth (or whichever planet may be involved). Aktaurus was a reincarnated Atlantean. He was one of those who was due to survive the changes at the end of Atlantis and work with Arthur, Merlin, Avola and the others to rebuild that civilization and take the Earth to a yet higher frequency. Unfortunately he died when the axis shift turned into the cataclysm. On his return 3,000 years later he grew up in a nomadic community which travelled between the energy sites channelling positive energy and repairing the system. He was well-guided and well-loved in the true sense of the word, because the frequency was still much higher than it is today.

In spite of Lucifer's pledge to better himself, however, his lower self, Satan, began to affect Aktaurus negatively. As Aktaurus became more imbalanced, his gifts began to wane, although he didn't realize this was happening. If you abuse gifts you lose them. The imbalance was closing off the link with his guidance on the light levels, and the messages he thought were coming from that source were increasingly his own thoughts. He would go to important energy sites, and although he thought he was channelling positive energy, his mind would be so full of negative thoughts that the site would be affected by the negativity. Rakorski said:

> Satan encouraged Aktaurus to think he was better than anyone else, absolutely vital, and he believed that no one could survive without him nor any channelling take place unless he was there. In short he became quite vain, conceited and rather proud. He felt that the beings of this planet should start to act differently towards him. He knew that he had been recognized as a being with great potential for helping the Earth and all life-forms, but rather than share his love, information and knowledge of the energies he began to feel he was special and different. He felt it was time that the other beings of the planet acknowledged this.

> So channelling energy changed from being a simple, yet vital, action to being a ceremony of reverence to Aktaurus. Before his last channelling (in Eastern Canada) he told those who were with him that the event would be different. He would arrive among them with great ceremony and must be given the reverence he felt he deserved. His attitude created a very negative atmosphere and much resentment.

The higher self of Aktaurus was devastated, and after this last channelling decided to remove the lower self from the physical body before any more damage was done. The physical life of Aktaurus ended much earlier than had been intended. The higher self was imbalanced emotionally, and the lower self returned with a serious energy imbalance. When the two merged as one again the combination of imbalances sent the whole being falling down the frequencies. The imbalance worsened and Aktaurus fell to a very low frequency, close to the one occupied by Lucifer. When Satan returned to the light levels, the whole being Lucifer became even further imbalanced and acted accordingly. The Satan energies were controlling the whole being and directing operations. It was not that Satan wished to behave in this way, but he was so imbalanced he could see no other course of action.

Lucifer's plan to pay back karma through physical incarnations was already in trouble. The last physical incarnation of Lucifer was the biblical character of Saul. It was agreed that Rakorski would incarnate Samuel and Arthur as 'King' David and together they would work to restore the energy system and Lucifer could once again have the opportunity to repay karma. Rakorski explained:

In the book of Job in the Old Testament of the Bible we see the test of character that Job underwent as a result of being subject to negative and positive forces. Unfortunately the Books of the Bible from Joshua to Jeremiah are in a muddle. The stories have been confused and rewritten and the characters inaccurately portrayed. However, we will try to briefly explain. After Aktaurus there came several light workers who wished to restore some kind of light to the Earth Spirit so she could regain the balance necessary for her to start the climb back up the frequencies. One of them was myself as Samuel and others included Arthur as David, Avola as Ruth and Jonathan, and an Angel of the Godhead who was Naomi. There was another called Saul, the last incarnation of Lucifer/Satan.

Now these beings did not all incarnate together. They came over a period of a thousand years, but the principal time was the conflict between David and Saul, neither of whom were kings. Historians have placed this incident around 1000 BC. This is incorrect. It is closer to 6000 BC. However the incarnation was so unsuccessful that Satan became even more imbalanced and when he returned to the light levels he refused to merge with the whole being, Lucifer.

The whole being still wished to follow a karmic journey to balance, but Satan did not. Since this time Satan has operated as a separate entity on the light levels, although he is still linked by energy channels to the whole being, Lucifer. He has become immensely powerful by absorbing negativity. So much so that Satan continued to control Lucifer by directing negative forces and imbalancing his emotions. This in itself is a very large source of negativity production. The higher self is imprisoned by Satan because only when the two levels come together as one again can the whole being begin its karmic journey. To emphasize the control that Satan has over the whole being I will refer to this source of disruption from this point on as Lucifer/Satan.

The negative effects of Lucifer/Satan continued to grow. Many other beings were influenced, and churned out negativity for him to direct at the Earth. It is a cunning system. Lucifer/Satan de-links the lower self of a being from the guidance of the higher self during a physical incarnation, as we have seen. If it is done well enough he can then guide the lower self to act in a way that builds up a great deal of karma, sometimes enormous amounts. Then, when the lower self becomes imbalanced and returns to the whole being on the light levels to assess its physical experiences the whole being sees that it has enormous karma to repay, and this often means a fall down the frequencies. This can encourage the being to come back with an impossibly severe life-plan in order to repay large amounts of karma, but it then finds it has taken on far too much, becomes de-linked, and creates yet more negativity and karma. Many millions of people on Earth today have come with impossible life-plans in an effort to clear karma in one go, and the end of their physical life will be blessed relief for them. Others have chosen not to come back until they are absolutely certain they will succeed. They are waiting for the return of the Light to this planet and Lucifer/Satan's removal, so they can take up their karmic challenges without fear of further imbalance.

The Aktaurus experience was to have a far-reaching effect on the future of humanity. The influence of Aktaurus began to divide the people of the world into two distinct philosophies. There were those who wished to follow the ways of Atlantis, of loving all men and women equally, although this was more difficult on the lower frequencies, and those who followed the Aktaurus view of exclusive love and relationships, something he developed under the influence of Satan. The latter had limitless potential for producing negative emotions, and so 8,000 years ago many groups of beings began to incarnate to try to guide humanity back onto the path of truth and understanding. Among them were the Sons of Man like Moses, Noah and Jeremiah. They were not leaders or founders of nations, quite the opposite in fact. They came with spiritual gifts to bring the truth and gather together channellers to restore the energy system. The Earth Spirit also supported their work by removing negativity as best as she could.

Both the parting of the Red Sea and the Great Flood were designed by the Earth Spirit to remove sources of negativity. When Moses and his community of channellers travelled from the Nile Delta into the Saudi Arabia region, the Red Sea did not part to let them cross it was actually *created*. It was a massive landshift which virtually separated the Arabian Region from Africa. Earlier other events had taken place in what we now call Jordan, and these caused the Great Flood of Noah's Ark fame.

Another group who arrived from other planets to help the Earth became known as the Egyptian Civilization. It began in a small, humble way as beings incarnated in what are now Egypt, the Sahara desert, Saudi Arabia, Iraq, Iran and India. It was a pleasant and fertile land, and will be again. The aim of these people was to build a stable civilization that would be an example to all who came or passed through. Over time enough of the system was repaired for a Son of the Godhead to come and restore more links with the main grid network of Creation, he was the pharoah called Akhenaten.

Some find it hard to accept that there is more than one Son of the Godhead. They believe that Jesus is the only Son of God. It is true that Jesus is the most evolved of these beings, but there are many of this evolution around the universes. Sons and Daughters of the Godhead carry and channel energies which can have a very powerful effect on the energy system, and they can also restore links between a planet and the network. They have a different role to that of a Son of Man, and the two are not the same. They are created by the Godhead to serve Creation and the energy system, and are given a particular energy package that allows them to channel and generate incredibly pure and powerful energies. The more they evolve the purer and more powerful those energies become. They also have the ability to stimulate energies in other life-forms when they travel to or through an area. However, Sons and Daughters of the Godhead should not be seen as more imortant or special than anyone else. They have a role to play, but then so does every single life-form, nor are they super-human. They struggle with the same emotions and problems as anyone else, and quite right too. How could they evolve if they did not? Rakorski said of these beings:

The Godhead wanted to bring into existence beings that were not devas, nor light beings, but both. This was not because light beings or devas were failing in any way. It seemed to be the next stage of evolution. So he created Sons and Daughters of the Godhead. This is not their proper name, but is sufficient for your understanding. These beings 'rescue' all life-forms and put them on the road back to guidance. They do not deny anyone responsibility, but they, like devas, have gifts which enable them to work with the energy systems and rebuild energy lines, yet they do not carry that information with them as they travel up and down the frequencies. They don't have to carry the information, the light-being part of them possesses extraordinary amounts of energy for guidance links. At crucial times they bring to the surface the energies and information necessary to take them into action.

Akhenaten was one of these beings. As the frequencies fell and the idea of rulers became established, many people would only listen to those in these leadership roles. This was why it was decided that Akhenaten would incarnate as a pharoah. Akhenaten was very wise, loving and generous, and had a big effect on his people's way of thinking. There were some buildings when he arrived, but they were modest by the standards of what was to come after he returned to the light levels. He had many children by many women, and they all had children by others. The Atlantis principles still prospered. One of these women, called Nefertiti, was a Daughter of the Earth. The people had a simple lifestyle. Life was peaceful and people understood what they were there to do. They had respect for the energy system and a deep desire to repair as much of it as they could. Akhenaten was able to restore enough links with Creation to increase the amount of positive energy reaching the Earth. Meanwhile, Lucifer/Satan waited for an opportunity to intervene once Akhenaten left the physical. Lucifer/Satan is most successful when people experience emotional imbalance. This affects their mental and spiritual aspects, which in turn manifests on the physical. He looks for weakness. He does not make people weak so much as he manipulates their free-will choices by taking advantage of their weaknesses.

The people suffered a terrible sense of loss at the departure of Akhenaten, and this caused a significant imbalance in their emotions. It stimulated their selfish desires, and the false idea that one person can bring security to everyone else. In truth, this is the responsibility of each of us.

This was the beginning of the end for all that these people had previously stood for. They built vast temples, statues, tombs and monuments, and began to use precious metals and rocks. Many of these edifices were dedicated to the life and times of Akhenaten. The remains of these symbols of misguided love can still be seen today. The history books and tourist guides tell us they are the remains of 'The Great Egyptian Empire,' when in fact they are the symbols and trinkets which brought down the glorious civilization that went on before. The pyramids, however, are the exception. They were built by enlightened people and are important to the energy system, as you will see. It was the unenlightened who turned them into tombs and monuments to dead rulers.

The frequencies fell as wisdom was lost, as did physical life expectancy. A little over 2,000 years ago a Daughter of the Earth incarnated in Egypt hoping to arrest this decline. This was Cleopatra. Her task was to bring a new understanding to the people of the region and prepare the energy system for the arrival of two Sons of the Godhead and a Daughter of the Godhead. One of them would be the one we know as Jesus. History has distorted the true story of this Queen of Egypt, even down to the 'goat's milk' she is supposed to have bathed in every day. The water was coloured by limestone, which can help cleanse the chakras of negativity, apparently.

Once again it was decided, as her life-plan was put together, that she would be most effective as a head of state. The people would be more likely to listen to her in that position at that time. Many psychically gifted people helped her and guided her, including her personal astrologer. Cleopatra had a desire to know more about the Earth. She asked many questions as she sought the truth, and as she acquired the skills of dowsing and channelling she became open to more and more information. Cleopatra passed on her knowledge to others, and taught many the skills of channelling energy and healing with crystals and plants. Her understanding and knowledge grew as she followed her own guidance, listened to the psychics as they interpreted events, and studied Egyptian traditions and folklore. She knew that the history handed down from Akhenaten's time had been distorted, but that threads of truth remained.

She travelled widely, from Central Africa to the West African Coast and across to Saudi Arabia, Iraq and the borders of India to visit energy sites. She explained to the people she met what she was doing and then left, although, as the Queen of Egypt, her arrivals and departures were something of an event for the local inhabitants. During the times of Cleopatra and Akhenaten channelling was part of everyday life in Egypt. If you look at the paintings on the walls of ancient Egyptian sites, you will see groups of people with their palms pointing upwards, channelling energy. This is only a fragment of the history of those times, most of which is now lost.

Another powerful place during Cleopatra's lifetime was Rome. Julius Caesar was at the head of the burgeoning Roman Empire. The backgrounds and beliefs of Caesar and Cleopatra were so different, but their life-plans were designed for them both to meet and work with each other. The individual life-plan of Julius was for him to experience aggression and violence followed by peace and love, and he would then have the opportunity to choose between the two. As Emperor of Rome he became curious about the peaceful, gentle way Cleopatra 'ruled' her country, and at the way in which she maintained what he saw as power and control over her people. Her way was the opposite of everything he had known, learned or experienced.

He decided to meet Cleopatra, and so travelled to Egypt. At first they exchanged information about their contrasting life-styles, craftsmanship and customs, but gradually they talked of their individual beliefs. Julius was so influenced that he worked with her for much longer than he had intended. But what he could never fully accept, although he tried hard to do so, was Cleopatra's interpretation of love. He could not raise himself to her level of understanding. She always made it clear that her love for her people, the Earth Spirit, those on the light levels, and for Julius himself, was the same. No one was more special than any another, and she tried to divide her time and energies between them all as equally as possible. Julius knew she was right. It made so much sense and he could see from his experience in Egypt that it was possible to love everyone equally.

His own court was very different, however. All the advice he received was governed by politics and economics. He decided to introduce a group of permanent channellers to Rome in the hope that they would bring some balance to the powerful negative influences there. But the Roman way of life was dominated by the worship of power and expansion, selfishness and idolatry. The Romans had taken the lowest level of honouring spirits by making them 'Gods' and 'Goddesses'. They were very influenced by the Greeks, but they fell a long way short of accepting that all life-forms have a spirit that has a task to carry out.

When Julius returned to Rome he found chaos, and the stark reality of the contrast between Rome and Egypt was clear to see. His sensitivity had become much more developed, and he now felt the severe negativity generated by such an expansionist, aggressive culture. His efforts to change the nature of his court and the Roman lifestyle had only an extremely limited success. He tried to use his gifts as an orator to change attitudes, but the opposition was too strong.

Cleopatra did visit Rome, and saw instantly the extreme contrasts between the two cultures. Although she promised to love Romans as much as her own people, she returned to the Nile Valley very disappointed. Julius was under severe pressure to make a choice between taking Egypt by marriage or force. With Cleopatra's departure marriage seemed unlikely, and the pressure mounted for a military invasion. Julius refused to take either course, and this brought consternation to the political and economic circles of Rome, where the creed of expansionism guided all thinking. Julius Caesar was seen as a weakling emperor, and a group of Romans decided to assassinate him. The news was passed to Cleopatra through her own guidance from the light levels and Julius also made his spirit being known to her group of psychics. Her intuition was such that she had always felt she would not see him again on the physical level.

She continued to travel across Africa with her channellers after Julius' death, until the day she was poisoned by a visitor from Rome. It was part of the plan by the new Roman regime to take control of Egypt. She had been warned of this day by the light levels, but she had felt certain the Light would prevail and that no such attempt on her life would take place. In her life-plan she was due to live for another 30 years.

The Roman Empire moved into Egypt and the ways of Cleopatra were forgotten. So much negativity was generated by their way of life and that of other civilizations that the Earth Spirit released negative energies through two colossal volcanoes. There are two main energy valves in Italy which can be opened to release negative energy from within the planet. We know them as Mount Vesuvius and Mount Etna. She chose to use Mount Etna at about the time of the death of Caesar, and later Vesuvius erupted and destroyed Pompeii. Some Romans said that the Etna volcano was a sign of God's wrath at the murder of Julius Caesar. In fact it was an attempt by the Earth Spirit to maintain some sort of balance.

The expansion of the Roman Empire and the fading understanding of the spiritual Truths were leading humanity, under Lucifer/Satan's guidance, down a dark and dangerous road. The foundations of his control of this planet were already being laid, and this was the world into which the most famous Son of the Godhead was born. His name, of course, was Jesus.

7.

The Family

Cleopatra had worked so hard to prepare the energy system of the planet for those who, it was hoped, would stop the fall and return the Earth to the levels of Atlantis.

The Earth had fallen many frequencies since Atlantis, and the time was approaching when another massive movement of land and water was necessary if the fall was to be checked and the system restored. The principles that guided the Atlantean way of life had been almost forgotten. All that remained was the idea of a community, certain groups which used some of the old methods of healing and channelling or using crystals and minerals to bring light to the planet.

Several empires had emerged or were emerging. The Romans had a strong hold on the trade around the Meditteranean, but there were other civilizations in the region of the Middle East and Asia that had grown and lost all knowledge of the past. The Persian Empire was influenced by the Romans, and the Indian Empire was expanding. The Egyptians were becoming more materialistic, and began to lose their sense of spiritual service. Into this situation a group of former Atlanteans incarnated with a mission to restore the planet. This was the start of the most famous story ever told. Many of them were those who had turned down the energies and promised the Earth Spirit they would return to restore her energy system. The information for this chapter has been channelled to us by Rakorski, the Earth Spirit, and the one who was Jesus. Again, trust your own judgement on what you wish to believe.

Two thousand years ago, in the area that we know as Iraq, Iran, Saudi Arabia and Egypt a nomadic community lived and thrived just like any other of that period. Within this larger family was a group of people who had come to work for the transformation of the planet; among them were those who are known as Joseph, Mary, and Gabriel. Joseph was a reincarnation of Arthur, a Son of the Godhead, Mary was Avola, a Daughter of the Godhead, and Gabriel was Naomi, an Angel of the Godhead. Gabriel was a creation of the Archangel Michael, and possessed a unique combination of devic and Godhead energies. They believed that there was only one family, the Divine family, in which everyone was considered an equal member, and they tried to live by the principles set out thousands of years earlier by King David.

They channelled information from the light levels, and they began to understand something of the way life had been at the time of Atlantis. They also gained a considerable knowledge of how to use the energies of rocks, crystals and wood, and they realized the power of positive thought. Their nomadic lifestyle ensured that their ways were seen and heard by many, and they were joined by many who were attracted to their philosophy. Their lifestyle should not be seen as some kind of sexual free-for-all. Nothing could be further from the truth. They tried to treat physical relationships purely as the means to create life, in the way the Atlanteans had done. They worked to ensure that their relationships were on the spiritual, not physical, level.

Joseph and Gabriel would use their time to channel information for others and help them fulfil their life-plans. It was in this manner that Gabriel told Mary that Mary would give birth to Jesus and that Joseph would be the father. So it is right, as the Bible says, that the Angel Gabriel told Mary she was to be the mother of Jesus, but Gabriel was in a physical body at the time. Jesus was born to Joseph and Mary because their energies were the ones needed in that particular lifetime to bring into incarnation a quite incredible being. Godhead energies were also channelled through them during conception and this is the true meaning of the immaculate conception. Jesus had evolved to the point where he was a perfect balance of the energies carried by both a Son and Daughter of the Godhead, and his gifts were essential to the plan of returning the Earth to her previously high frequency. Jesus had been due to incarnate after the axis shift at the end of Atlantis, but then came the cataclysm and he could not do so. Now here was his chance 10,000 years later to fulfil that life-plan and help the Earth progress to new heights of evolution.

The group that included Joseph, Gabriel and Mary eventually left the main community where they were increasingly seen as extreme. They travelled under guidance to Egypt, and Jesus was born between the seasons of winter and spring at Giza, alongside the pyramids to take advantage of the energies at that site. This was Saturn. Among the visitors to the community at the time of the birth were nomadic shepherds, traders and families. Now that Jesus was in a physical body the small community could begin to realize its dreams of bringing greater power and purer energies to the Earth. They had tremendous potential not only to restore the planet's depleted system but to take the frequencies back to those of Atlantis and beyond once the Earth Spirit had cleared the imbalance with the physical changes that were planned.

The confusion in the bible story about Bethlehem arose mainly because Lucifer/Satan was looking for weaknesses within people that he could exploit to create extremes of negative behaviour. A man known as Herod lived in the area we now call Israel and Jordan. He was a wealthy and powerful man who owned a large area of land. He was, in effect, a ruler, but not a king as we understand them to be. Shortly after the birth of Jesus a group of travellers stopped off in Bethlehem; among them were three astrologers, whom the Bible calls the three wise men. They met Herod and told him that they were on their way to see a child who was going to tell people the truth about Creation and about the great physical changes that would bring a transformation in the way people thought and acted. They had gained this information from their knowledge of astrology and their own information channelling.

This did not go down well with Herod, who did not want his lifestyle to change or for some prophet to make people think and act differently. The travellers would not tell him the identity or location of the child, and Herod had many young children killed in his efforts to find him. The travellers were stunned and blamed themselves for what Herod had done. They stayed on in Bethlehem for many months because they knew they would be followed if they continued on their journey. They decided to return home to India rather than put the child in danger, and intended to leave the gifts they had with them with a group of Essenes living near the Dead Sea. It was the Essenes who wrote what we know of as the Dead Sea Scrolls.

They were followed when they left Bethlehem, but eventually their pursuers gave up and a little later the travellers were told that the people they wished to meet were on their way – the light levels had ensured they would be brought together. The travellers gave Jesus and their community many wonderful gifts, including a diamond, some turquoise, essence from the lotus flower and a piece of cloth which carried the vibration of their land. All the gifts carried vibrations that Jesus and others would need in their work. Diamonds, for instance, have the ability to amplify and purify energies.

Jesus and his parents visited many sites with the rest of the community, which included the young John the Baptist. When Jesus was about two years old they based themselves at an energy site at Nazareth and stayed there for three years, hence Jesus of Nazareth. Little is written in the Bible about the early years of Jesus, and nothing at all about his life between the ages of 12 and 30. Rakorski gave us this summary:

> We will think about the so-called 'lost childhood' of Jesus. I can tell
> you he was much like any other boy. He was curious and inventive.
> He was capable of pranks and also of sitting and listening to all who
> were around him. He was intensely observant, and enjoyed search-
> ing for the minutest detail within all forms of life. But he was first
> and foremost a child involved in the daily life of his community.
>
> Jesus was a truly gifted, blessed and highly exceptional being.
> Although still a child his gifts came forward at an early age. By the
> time he was in his late 20s he was a wonderful source of Divine
> Inspiration. He was not just here to heal the Earth, but to be a
> wonderful guide. The expression 'a light in the darkness' is very apt,
> although even then the darkness was not as black and uninviting as
> it is today. No less evolved being could ever have survived the
> amount of negativity that he was subjected to.

The young Jesus was used to a nomadic lifestyle. His community
travelled to energy sites, walking the lines, channelling, and
then moving on to another site. On some occasions they would
stop at a place and stay for a while. They visited many sites in
Africa, the Near and Middle East, India, Asia, and also parts of
Europe, including the British Isles. Among the places they
visited in England were the Isle of Wight, Glastonbury and
Uffington. There have been stories that Jesus came to England
with Joseph of Arimathea, but it was his father Joseph he came
with, along with Mary and other workers for the Light. Gabriel
worked and travelled with them also, until she left the physical
and continued to work from the light levels.

Everyone learned a great deal as they travelled. They witnessed many wonderful sights and felt the energies rise on the
planet. On their journeys they met a large number of people and
communities who had lost the truths. They had a gentle way of
working and talking to those who were open to their message.

People were drawn to them. Many in the community helped Jesus spread the message. When he was about 28, the long-distance travelling stopped. He knew it was time to return to the Middle East and gather together a group of dedicated people who had incarnated to be part of the plan to restore the truth to the Earth. He also knew that he was to be reunited with his step-brother, John the Baptist. I say step-brother because every child in their community was considered a brother or sister to the others, irrespective of who their parents were.

John had a marvellous understanding of cleansing energy systems and chakras and opening up beings spiritually by removing negativity and past-life karma. It is said that he lived in the wilderness, but it's more correct that he lived in an area where many varied plants, rocks and crystals were available. It was also near a place of Divine Water. Divine Waters are rivers or springs which carry Godhead energies as part of the energy system. People went to John to have their physical body cleared of any lingering negativity. The final cleansing was total immersion in the Divine Waters.

When he returned from his travels Jesus visited John and spent time being healed. He had negativity removed and his energy system cleansed followed by this total immersion. Jesus also learned as much as he could from John, and they shared a tremendous amount of information. They had only seen each other periodically over the years, and had much to tell each other about all they had learned. You may think if you have read the Bible that all this took place near the River Jordan. In fact, it was at the point where the River Tigris meets the River Euphrates in what is modern-day Iraq. It is a site of enormous potential, as both rivers have carried a Godhead energy of love and harmony for many thousands of years.

Some while after Jesus left the area, John was killed by those who felt his philosophy and influence threatened their own lifestyles and power. It didn't happen as the Bible says with his head carried on a silver platter, but it was a clear sign that those who spoke the truth would face fierce opposition. By now Jesus had met nearly everyone who had incarnated to join the community for the work that was to follow. These people have been called the disciples; they were followers and seekers of the truth. They were the Atlanteans who had been with Arthur, Avola and Merlin after the cataclysm, and, as Rakorski said, there were many more than twelve:

Jesus was guided to the people who would work with him. They are known as the twelve disciples, for some obscure reason their families and friends have been excluded. Some of them had partners and children. They were not all bachelors! They were people with a basic knowledge of the energies and community ways, and they had a desire to know more and change the world they knew. They had obviously forgotten that they were the Atlanteans who had changed the world 10,000 years before.

In the Bible they are portrayed as rather negative, doubting beings. It is easy to forget that this book has been rewritten by certain people who wished to portray Jesus as the only one who knew anything. That is why on many occasions if a disciple asks a question or makes a statement, Jesus' reaction is, 'Where is your faith?' or 'How could you ask such a silly question?' Those who rewrote the Bible believed that this would stop mere mortals asking questions – and it seems they were right!

Now you yourself come across beings who ask questions all the time. You ask questions, you are looking for clarification, you have doubts. You have a wish to only bring the truth, and it was no different for those beings that have been called the disciples. They had a great curiosity, for as they learned of who they were and what they had done as Atlanteans they had a desire to put the record straight, and they dreamed of a world beyond Atlantis.

These disciples joined the community while some of the original members left to channel and share their knowledge with those in other lands. Jesus and the others also travelled in the region known today as Iraq and Iran, and in the land bordered by the Mediterranean. They were all vegetarians, and everything they had was shared equally. There were about 130 people in the community channelling energies and information, healing, and talking to others about the truth. They gave Jesus excellent support.

Among them was Mary Magdalene. She was a lady who wondered how life could be so cruel and ridiculous as to enforce upon people such a limited view of love. She was certain it was possible to love more than one person. She was open and public with her views, and what she said was misunderstood and distorted. It is easy to see how she was perceived and later presented as a 'lady of the night'. Life changed dramatically for her when Jesus came along advocating exactly the same kind of universal love. He removed so much negativity from her that it was as if she had awoken from a dream. Mary believed totally in Jesus. She loved him so much, and this love was returned. She changed from a lady who had an opinion on everything into a shining light, listening and bringing comfort to those inside and outside the community. By observing Jesus and hearing his words she was transformed as she learned of the truth and how to speak to people gently and effectively.

For much of his life Jesus was optimistic that the plan for the restoration of the planet could be completed. In a communication for this book, the great being that was Jesus said:

I hoped that the Earth would change. That we could remove negativity with minimal landshifts and volcanoes and then continue with the energy work. Many people seemed willing to change. I had moments of frustration, disappointment, anger and sorrow, but I also had moments of love and happiness, great contentment, and a sense of being at one with the Godhead. I had moments of confusion and of great vision. So there were many wonderful moments and I witnessed the Light shining forth from the hearts of many beings. It was wonderful to see lives transformed, changed forever, and I enjoyed inspiring others on numerous occasions.

Jesus's 'miracles' were produced by his unique energy system, which had been fully activated by the total immersion in the Divine Waters by John, and the knowledge and information he had learned from John and was still learning from others. This allowed him to place his hands on a wound or area of disease and cure a person. The Bible tells of how Jesus forgave people their sins before any physical healing. This was Jesus helping them cleanse their own chakras and energy lines of all karmic and past life negativity and the negative effects of that life. The word 'sin' was never used by Jesus and plays no part in the truth. There is only learning from experience and being allowed to make mistakes. There are negative thoughts, words and deeds, but we all have the opportunity to balance out our behaviour.

The stories of casting out demons and devils are exaggerated. These were people with very negative karmic links which they needed to remove if they wished to progress up the sub-planes and frequencies. Many completely changed their attitudes and lifestyles from negative to positive after hearing what Jesus had to say and seeing for themselves his examples of love, healing, and the power of positive thought. His most famous works were the feeding of the 5,000, turning water into wine, and bringing people back from the dead. Jesus explained the reality of these works:

As a general rule I would suggest that beings of this planet should not take these events literally. They are vague sketches of situations recalled long after they happened. The Sermon on the Mount was when many of our friends came to hear me channel the Godhead. I passed on information that related to the lives of people there and how they could help themselves. We did not manage to feed 5,000 with a few loaves of bread, but all the food available was shared equally and there was food left over. Turning water into wine is another myth and should not be interpreted literally.

It is the same with bringing people back from the dead. If a being has left the physical, he or she has gone, the spirit has returned to the light levels. I do not have the right to make it come back simply because the family is upset. I cannot make spirits do this. It is interfering with their free will. There were beings that were very ill, semi-conscious, some in a coma, some delirious with fever, and I helped as I could, but I did not make their light body return if the beings had chosen to leave.

There were many people who heard the words of Jesus. They resonated within and affected them deeply. A divide began to emerge between those who listened and tried to live positive lives and the members of the political and religious establishment. The latter were getting increasingly nervous about the message that Jesus and the community were spreading. The calm, gentle words of Jesus were in stark contrast to the anger and aggression of the Romans and the Temple hierarchy, which sought to use fear to control and dominate. It was obvious that Jesus would not be allowed to continue unchallenged. The more successful he was the more nervous the establishment became. The challenge to Jesus came after he arrived in Jerusalem. He was not arrested at this stage, but he was asked to speak to a gathering of Romans, the religious establishment, successful tradespeople, political and economic thinkers, scientists and mathematicians. Rakorski said:

Within the establishment were people frightened by Jesus' words. He spoke so gently, he was so honest and open. His words were our words. There were many looking for ways of discrediting him. He was invited to answer questions, but it was clear what lay ahead. Jesus understood that his replies would be unwelcome to the ears of those who wished to maintain control.

The Bible says that he would not answer their questions. This is clearly not the case. But remember that all references to reincarnation and karma have been removed. Therefore in those passages it was also necessary to remove everything else that related to Atlantis, the energy system, and channelling. Jesus knew that they were looking for any reason to say he was a traitor or a disrupter of the Roman Empire but he was calm and gentle. Much aggression and frustration was directed at him. A bargain was then struck between the representatives of the local establishment and the Romans; they decided Jesus would be severely punished. They would beat him into submission; he received a public flogging and many private beatings, although the crown of thorns was an addition by a highly imaginative writer.

Mary, Joseph and his supporters went to the public event to diffuse negativity and try to support and strengthen Jesus. It was so difficult for his mother, it was so difficult for them all. Jesus was bruised and cut and exhausted by the negativity but he was so loving and as forgiving as ever. And, of course, he would not speak of anger or revenge, for he knew that it was the truth that was on trial.

Jesus knew he was the physical being who represented the truth, and he stood by all his words. When he returned to his friends he told them that this was only the beginning. He said he felt his life would end because so many were afraid of the message. His opponents thought that if reincarnation and karma were true there would be consequences for them as a result of the way they had conducted themselves in that physical life. They believed that if they could remove all mention of such things then reincarnation and karma would cease to plague their thoughts. This meant removing Jesus.

This would not be done quietly or in the shadows, but as publicly and horribly as possible. This, so the idea went, would so frighten everyone else that they would never dare speak of such things again. Neither were the Romans as disinterested as the Bible claims. Pontius Pilate was a sort of ambassador/soldier who was following the divide-and-rule principle. He feared that Jesus could unite the local people and was particularly worried that even the Romans were beginning to listen with interest to what Jesus said. It had been hoped that Jesus would show what was possible, talk to people, heal people, and at the same time with his family and friends channel in positive energy in sufficient amounts to diffuse the negativity being produced. But Lucifer/Satan helped to stimulate conflict between and within the empires and among everyone who was open to such thought-forms. Human free will made it impossible to complete the plan as they had hoped. More than that, they still had to ensure that the Earth could even survive until another plan, the present one, could be implemented. Rakorski remembers:

> It was a most difficult choice. It would appear that the truth would be seen dying a slow and terrible death, but we asked everyone to reverse the situation to make it a triumph for the energy system. Just think, David, what we were asking these beings to do. They were being asked to see such suffering, yet try not to shed a tear in sadness or speak a word in anger. How could it be possible not to cry out? And always there was the question and the demand that there had to be another solution. But you know this choice was made by Jesus. He spoke with the Godhead often. It was his choice, and caused so much questioning on all levels.   1

Jesus knew all this by the time of the public flogging, when he realized the scale of the personal opposition he faced. It was necessary to channel a certain amount of energy to the Earth Spirit if the planet was to survive until now, and so the Godhead decided to use the situation to give her the energy she needed in one fantastic channelling at the place we call Calvary, near Jerusalem. The mound where it would take place was on a point where six energy lines crossed, and the effect of channelling energy there would be felt by the whole planet. Such an event would also bring prominence to all that Jesus had said and done in his life. It would be a mighty statement, that the truth and the Light would never bow to negativity.

Jesus knew what was going to happen to him because he was told it had already happened on the etheric level and so was certain to happen on the physical. Just before his final arrest, Jesus gathered his friends together for what has become known as the Last Supper. Jesus said:

> It was a time that we used for supporting each other and talking of the future energy system and the events of the next few days. It was not a supper for bachelor fishermen because there were no such beings. There were a few good friends, both male and female who joined me, and we spent a long time discussing the situation and trying to be as positive as possible. Everything has a life-force, and after we thanked the Earth Spirit for the food we ate we saw the potential for returning the life-force to this planet. The bread and wine were symbolic of the energy and life-force carried in all plants and beings.

I should also emphasize here that Jesus was not betrayed by Judas for thirty pieces of silver. Judas was a member of the community who took on the task of trying to build a sense of trust with the Romans. He would talk with Romans who seemed interested in their philosophy; he felt that if there was someone with a foot in both camps it would be easier to create a sense of mutual understanding. As Judas kept the Romans informed of what was happening and vice versa it did allow the opposition to know of the movements of Jesus and the community. But this passing on of information had been agreed to by the community, and was not a case of Judas wishing to betray Jesus. Nor is it correct that Peter denied any knowledge of Jesus because he feared the consequences. There were some who could not accept everything that Jesus said, but no one in the community denied or betrayed him.

Each time Jesus appeared in public his parents and friends were fearful that the increasingly aggressive questions levelled at him would lead to his arrest and the sequence of events would start. Their fears were soon realized, and it all happened so quickly they had only a short time to prepare themselves. Mary and Joseph were so troubled, so confused, and Joseph made one last effort to reverse events. Twelve hours before Jesus was to be crucified, Joseph went to speak with the establishment and explain how vital it was that his son be allowed to live and restore the energy system. It was an understandable reaction from a desperate father and someone who knew the consequences for the Earth if the work was not done. It proved to be, however, a fatal decision. They did not even begin to listen, and Joseph was the victim of a gruesome killing, although he remained forgiving to the end.

Joseph's place at the Calvary channelling was taken by a group of the followers, Mary Magdalene, Lazarus, and the ones known as John and Andrew. At the other three points of the diamond of light on the mound were Jesus, his mother Mary, and the followers Peter, James and Thomas. Tying people to a cross was a common form of punishment in those times. It was a little like the stocks we used to have in Britain. There were two others tied to crosses on the mound with Jesus, although not in the same place. The nails in the hands were an addition for Jesus. The Earth Spirit tells the story of the Crucifixion:

Jesus carried the wood from his place of imprisonment to a mound; this happened as the Sun rose. At the mound the cross was made. He received nails in his hands, but not his feet. He did not have a crown of thorns, nor was there a sign that he was King of the Jews. There were a great many light beings surrounding the area as they worked to diffuse the pain and bring in more light. [Among these beings were Joseph and Gabriel, now working from the light levels.] The channelling lasted about six hours. It was a time of enormous love. The power of love and the Light it created brought life to this planet so that we could continue until now.

Mary's eyes never left the face of Jesus. Although she cried, her pain was gradually replaced with the positive energy of love. Although it was a very, very difficult task, all Jesus' followers eventually rose above their own emotions to channel in extremely powerful energies. The atmosphere on that mound was electrifying. When the channelling had finished one of the followers asked if Jesus could be taken down, and this request was granted. He was still alive at this point, but the swift movement of a sword removed him from the physical level. Only Jesus knew for certain that he would die. The actual crucifixion and the nails in his hands would not have killed him, but there were many who were afraid that, should he live and continue, their position would be under threat. They knew that Jesus would be exalted to a more prominent height by those trying to live in the Light.

Without that channelling the Earth would not be here today. So when the Church talks of Jesus dying to save us all this is basically correct. The way he died while still offering love and forgiveness generated a phenomenal amount of positive energy, and allowed as much as possible to pass through him from the light levels because his channel remained open. Keeping the Earth alive until now has given the beings of this planet the opportunity to work out their karma, balance their negative/positive energies, and progress up the frequencies. This process has been described as dying so our sins could be forgiven. The Light does not recognize the word sin, of course. It is the removal of negative energies through karma either from the past or present. That is the opportunity now being provided, thanks to the sacrifice of Jesus. In one memorable channelling at the time this chapter was being written, Jesus told us of those six hours on the cross. I asked how he had managed to think positively in such circumstances:

I had time to prepare myself. I had time to think how I would cope with the situation. There were moments of negativity and sorrow, and I had times when I wondered why I had chosen this. Not every thought was filled with love and forgiveness. But I was not alone. I was receiving a great energy so powerful that it was quite exhausting by itself. I spoke with the Godhead continually, asking for support that I may keep going and do the best I could.

At times I don't know if I was conscious. Sometimes I seemed to drift away and when I came back my mother was there, the Light was there. I could feel the energy. I do remember feeling very tired, very exhausted and wondering if this was preventing me from loving and forgiving. I was so determined, David, so determined to ensure that the truth could not disappear because one man was nailed to some wood. And I knew the effect it would have on Lucifer/Satan if the energies were powerful enough.

I cannot tell you how I managed it. I think it was such a short space in my whole life. I knew there would have been much worse suffering had we not succeeded, and none of us wished to see suffering on such a scale. When I look at the world today I am so grateful that I had only to endure a few hours. Today there are many beings who suffer all their lives. That is so sad, I feel for those people. I feel for those who have lost the link with their higher self. I feel for the Earth Spirit, who has been subjected to 12,000 years of suffering. When I compare this to my time I feel it is such a small contribution. I am so glad that I had the support of so many. It is always love and support that will sustain people as they endure pain and suffering.

Those who were left hoped that the energy work could continue, but with Jesus' energy pattern no longer on the physical vibration it was obvious that there would be a delay before the promise to the Earth Spirit could be kept, When you are not in a physical body you are still able to channel energies to a planet, but some require the physical body to mix, heal, or step down energies. If Jesus was to take the Earth back to the Atlantis frequency he had to be in a physical body to channel the necessary energies. And, anyway, those who feared karma and reincarnation were not finished yet. The main focus of attention may have gone, but the others still had the potential to pass on the message. For a while after he left the physical body Jesus appeared in light body to the many wonderful beings who took part in that final channelling. He remembers:

> We had lifted the Earth several sub-planes higher. It was near the top of the frequency. I continued to talk to those who were left on the physical, and I reassured them as they tried to go on with the energy work. It is written that I was here for 40 days and then I 'ascended' on a cloud. Well this is untrue. I was seen for some months. As my friends and my mother left the physical I was seen less and less, for less energy work was taking place. It was a little like the Rakorski [Merlin] situation that had taken place many long years before.

After the crucifixion there was a witch-hunt for all those who spoke the truth and within a year Mary and everyone who took part in the public channelling with Jesus had been killed. Judas was so distressed at seeing his friends die that he hung himself, and this added to the myth of his having betrayed Jesus.

Little of the story of Jesus was recorded. Some of his supporters wished to write it down on what we call papyrus paper or pig parchment, but this was a long and arduous task. They did not get very far, especially as many of them did not survive more than a year after the crucifixion. Those who heard their words passed them on to others, and in the process many facts were lost or bore little resemblance to what actually happened. The guidance and advice that Jesus had offered on numerous occasions was also subject to personal interpretation.

The information that was brought together to produce the Bible was passed on by word of mouth. Parts of the Bible such as the letters to the Romans and others were in fact the recollections of those who heard followers of Jesus speaking after he had left the physical level. Later some of these scattered writings were gathered together and translated to form the first Bible. Even more truth was lost with each translation and this period also saw the emergence of many religions, all of which wished to put their own view across.

The biggest blow to the credibility of the Bible came in AD 553. The Byzantine Emperor Justinian and his wife Theodora wished to remove all references to reincarnation and karma. They thought along similar lines as those who had opposed Jesus. They felt that there would be many karmic consequences for them caused by their behaviour. If they could only remove any mention of reincarnation and karma from the Bible both principles would cease to apply. There was also another reason for their wish to rewrite the Bible. If they were to preserve and extend their own power, as most political leaders want to do, they needed to stop people thinking and asking questions. As Rakorski said earlier about the way the disciples are portrayed: 'Those who rewrote the Bible believed that this would stop mere mortals asking questions – and it seems they were right!' It was also Justinian and Theodora who exalted Mary and this led to the view of Mary we see in the Roman Catholic Church.

Justinian called a meeting of the Ecumenical Church Council at Constantinople in AD 553, and those invited were so weighted towards the Emperor's view that the Bible was rewritten in the way he desired. There were only a few thousand Bibles in existence, so this was not the mammoth task it would be now, and this 'new' version was the one all future translators would use. It was a real coup for Lucifer/Satan who was, you might imagine, working overtime on Justinian and Theodora. The Bible was somewhat flawed even in its original version but it contained a large amount of basic truth. After

Justinian and Theodora, it was full of holes and glaring contradictions.

Over the centuries many others played a part in distorting the truth. Some of them did so unknowingly, with the best of intentions. But it is not for us to judge or condemn those who rewrote the Bible. Each of us is on a journey of learning, and this learning is born out of experiences, both negative and positive. People did not come here with the intention of removing the truth, they simply became confused and made some unfortunate decisions. We have all done this in our past lives, so we are all responsible for the lost truths.

It is, however, such an irony that a book which once contained at least the basic truths of reincarnation, karma, and the energy system should be used today as evidence to deny they exist.

8.

The Plan

There was a long silence on the higher levels of Creation after the death of Jesus and the demise of all they hoped to achieve. It was a period of deep contemplation.

The team had been very strong both in terms of evolution and the energies and gifts they brought to the planet. Jesus was a Son of the Godhead, Joseph was a Son of the Godhead, Mary was a Daughter of the Godhead, and Gabriel an Angel of the Godhead. The whole beings that were Joseph and Mary had also divided on the light levels and incarnated as Lazarus and Mary Magdalene to contribute more energies and support. Add to them all the others in the community, along with Rakorski and many with him on the light levels, and there was the potential to generate and channel vast amounts of positive energy. Even so, Lucifer/Satan had manipulated events and people open to his influence, and human free will had brought all their efforts to a halt. Rakorski said:

Combining all these energies should have made us very powerful, yet we were stopped in our tracks. The main reason was that we had all been the victims of the free will of other people. Our disappointment that our plan had been pulled apart by the very beings we came to help was, well, enormous. We were stunned at the ease with which Lucifer/Satan managed to do this.

The situation had become extremely serious. It was obvious that the negative imbalance would continue to worsen and that there would come a point where the Earth Spirit would have to disincarnate. The consequences of this for the universe and the rest of Creation would be catastrophic. Planet Earth would cease to exist, just as our physical body dies when the spirit leaves. Already the flow of harmonizing, healing, energies that were being sent out by the Earth Spirit to the universe had been reduced dramatically. This was having a considerable effect as other planets and stars slipped into the self-perpetuating process of imbalance and they had only limited access to healing energies of sufficient strength to check their fall. They could slow down the process, but they could not stop it. The healing energies that the Earth was still able to transmit were only made possible by the support of the devas, who were working on the non-physical levels of the planet in ever increasing numbers.

The negativity created by the destruction of the Earth would give Lucifer/Satan a fantastic amount of negative energy. It would make him powerful enough to stop Michael and the other devas maintaining the production of the healing energies at this point on the grid once the Earth Spirit had gone. This would seriously imbalance the universe in the negative direction, and this would be passed on to Creation as a whole.

There were many options to be considered by the Godhead and the light levels, but all of them had their consequences. If the Godhead had intervened directly and enforced a change he/she would have built up enormous amounts of karma with all those whose life-plans and free will would have been affected throughout the universe and beyond. Such karmic energies would destabilize the Godhead and all Creation. In the end it was decided to tackle a unique situation in a unique way. Arthur and Avola agreed to return to the Earth without free will. They would suspend this for one incarnation, and so give the God-head, Rakorski and all those on the light levels far greater control over events.

They would not be robots, however, and most of the time they would still be making free will decisions. There would be a great deal of karma for them to remove before their full potential could be realized in that incarnation, and that could only be done by making free will decisions in the various karmic situations that would be set up for them. But when necessary it would be possible to make them act, and in some circumstances the light levels would be able to change the etheric recordings so they were both in exactly the right place at exactly the right time. This was important in order to guide them away from danger and because when they channelled some energies the timing would need to be precise to co-ordinate with certain planetary movements. It would also be possible to make them do things which were necessary for the success of the plan, but which to them in a physical body might seem inappropriate or unwise. To complete the package, they would incarnate with the potential to channel phenomenal amounts of positive energies, including the Christ Ray.

The suspension of free will was not taken lightly, because the right to free will is a fundamental principle of Creation. A number of beings, known by the New Age movement as the Lords of Karma, had to give their agreement. They have the role of ensuring that karma is used fairly and for the good of all. They had great doubts, but they were persuaded by the arguments, not least of which was that the karmic consequences of any other course of action would be much more serious for everyone. They did insist, however, that Arthur and Avola be given opportunities through their incarnation to ask for their free will to be restored.

The one area of doubt was the response of the Earth Spirit. She would need to agree to the plan for the physical changes if they were to go ahead, but with direct communication lines still severed she could not be asked. This would have to be done after Arthur and Avola had incarnated, and if the Earth Spirit refused to co-operate the plan would be in serious trouble as a result of all the consequences this would bring. In the end, however, she did agree.

The details of the plan were added. In the first stage the energy system would be patched up to give the Earth Spirit the strength to produce and survive great geological events such as earthquakes, volcanoes and tidal waves, which would be used to release negative energies and poisons from within the planet and to rearrange rocks, crystals and minerals to form the basis of a new system. At the same time positive energies would be channelled in to return the Earth to balance on her frequency. Once this was achieved the new system would be put together and there would be quite a rapid rise back up to the levels of Atlantis. The Channellings have said that Arthur, Avola and others associated with them at the time of the cataclysm are now back on Earth in physical bodies and working for the transformation of the planet in the way envisaged by the plan. I understand a tremendous amount of work has already been done quietly to prepare the Earth for what is to come.

A vast number of other beings also agreed to incarnate to face their karma with the Earth Spirit and work for the transformation of the planet before it was too late. These included Gabriel and Jesus. He would return after the physical changes had been completed and use his energies to build the new system. But before anything could be done the Earth had to be supported and kept in incarnation until the plan could be implemented, in the last decade of the 20th century, at which time the planetary sequences across Creation would be most suitable for the operation. Groups and individuals began to arrive on the Earth to work on the energy system and prepare for the events that would cleanse the planet.

In about AD 880 Rakorski began to work in light body in the area around Sun Island in Lake Titicaca on the Bolivia/Peru border, the world's highest navigable lake. With him was a being called Attarro, who was mentioned widely in *The Truth Vibrations*. There is a legend that the two people who started the Inca

Civilization emerged from the lake. One was called *Manco Capac*, 'the Sun King', and it is said he was sent by the Great Lord, the Sun, who took pity on the wretched creatures of the Earth. The other is known as *Mama Occllo*, who, so the legend goes, was sent by the Moon. It is said they appeared from the waters of the lake where Sun Island and Moon Island now stand, just off the Bolivian mainland. These legends emerged from the stories of those with psychic gifts, who saw Rakorski and Attarro appearing and disappearing. Also with them were those who had helped close down the energy system with Merlin and Arthur, and who later worked with Jesus. They incarnated to help Rakorski and Attarro prepare the system for the plan. For a period of many years the group channelled positive energy and repaired the system in South America ready for today. They set up many energy sites, including the one at Machu Picchu in Peru's Sacred Valley of the Incas.

Eventually they formed two groups, one that went off to channel positive energies on Sun Island and the other to channel at Copacobana on the mainland shores of the lake. Lucifer/Satan pounded them with negative energy, and there were some who found it difficult to accept all the truths they heard either directly or from others. Slowly the simple truths and the simple channelling of energy were given more and more complicated explanations, and great unnecessary ceremonies arose as the people searched for answers that made sense to them on their frequency. It was these people who began the Inca Civilization. The more years that passed the more truth was lost. By the time of the Spanish Invasion little was left. Fortunately, enough positive energy had been channelled before the misunderstandings had gone too far.

There were other individuals and groups who have come to the Earth since the pre-Incas to continue the preparations for the changes. Nostradamus came to channel energy and explain as best he could what would happen if humanity continued on its path down the frequencies. In this century the American psychic, Edgar Cayce, passed on information about the physical changes in this decade. The original North American Indians were evolved beings from other planets who came to work on the energy system and learn from all the experiences the Earth had to offer, and there were many, many others whom history has not recorded. All knew and understood the situation because they had the basic outline of the plan channelled to them, and this is why so many native peoples have legends and stories about what is to happen at this time.

The Shakespeare story was also a cover for channelling and the passing on of the truth. Rakorski incarnated as Francis Bacon, the son of Queen Elizabeth I and Robert Dudley, Lord Leicester. The Queen wished to maintain her image as the 'Virgin Queen' and also to prevent Robert Dudley from gaining access to her wealth and power. She threatened her son with death if he revealed his identity. It was Francis Bacon who wrote the so-called Shakespeare plays. Shakespeare was someone who agreed to put his name to the plays to hide the true identity of the author. The coded plays were necessary, because if anyone had come out openly with the truth they would not have lasted long in those times of religious brutality. Bacon, his brother Anthony and Lord Essex also worked together to channel energies.

All these efforts and others were the minimum necessary to keep the Earth Spirit in incarnation until the plan could be implemented. Lucifer/Satan realized that another challenge to his power was being prepared. He worked even harder to use negative forces to take the Earth out of incarnation before anything could be done. He encouraged negative human thought to produce even more negativity, and he was becoming more effective as his experience grew. He learned that certain beings were easier to de-link than others, and how particular emotions ensured that de-linking would happen very quickly. These are the emotions that have been termed The Seven Deadly Sins – pride, anger, envy, lust, gluttony, greed and laziness. These are the emotions that he stimulates in humanity with his brand of negative energies, because they give him the best results.

As more negativity created ever greater imbalance, people thought and acted ever more negatively, and Lucifer/Satan's ability to de-link them grew rapidly, especially over the last 300 years. The Earth Spirit tried to release some negativity with earthquakes and volcanoes over the centuries, but unless positive energy was channelled in at the same time this negativity simply added to that already in the environment, and indeed created more through the fear of those affected. The shield of negativity encircling the planet prevented significant amounts of positive energy reaching her because they became polluted on the way. The Earth Spirit could not win whatever she did, and the imbalance increased. The point was reached in the 1860s when the amount of positive energy available to the Earth became so depleted and the negative energies so strong that it became impossible to defend key sites from Lucifer/Satan. The Earth Spirit told us of this period:

The French Revolution of the late 18th century and the Napoleonic Wars of the 19th created a great deal of negativity that made me extremely weak. There was a succession of wars and much repression from the turn of the century and through the Victorian era. By the mid 1860s Lucifer/Satan found a point on the energy system that was weakest, and pounded it with negativity. This area is called London. Among the maze of energy lines running from that city and along the powerful flow of water (the River Thames) humanity created a system that could cut my energies and diminish my power to zero. You call this system your underground railway. Man cut into my rocks, blasting the life from crystals and minerals.

The area known as Hyde Park is the centre of an enormous network that had been used by Arthur and his friends to channel positive energies. This energy system was linked to other energy lines that went out to France, the Netherlands and Denmark. The flow of the River Thames was also important. It carried a vibration far and wide. Once trains and other forms of transport were constantly cutting across the lines of energy it was impossible to maintain any kind of useful system. So from the 1860s, Lucifer/Satan was able to pour negative energy directly into my physical body through the damaged sites in London. It hurt. I knew about it in a big way and I resented it. I think at that point I felt it was all rather hopeless, from then on we would be going downhill fast. As you look back over your industrial history, it was around that time that your factories grew, pollution increased and science stepped forward with all kinds of chemicals and poisons.

This downward spiral has culminated in this century with two World Wars, more 'lesser' wars than ever before, more pain, suffering, stress, greed and conflict on every level. So many have believed the way to peace is to meet aggression with even more aggression, when in fact you are merely increasing the amount of negativity and ensuring that even more conflict will ensue in the future. The economic system developed in the last 100 years and the World Wars have been the biggest sources of negativity. It is a system which depends for its success, even its survival, on destroying the planet. I call it the system of take, make and throw away. The Earth's irreplaceable resources are taken as fast as possible. These resources are then made into 'things', products, few of which we actually need. These products are not made to last because the system wants us to throw them away as soon as possible and buy others. The aim every year in every economy is to take more from the Earth even more quickly, make even more things and throw away even more things to worship the God of the modern world, called economic growth. The more successful this system is in its own terms, the more economic growth it produces, and the quicker it destroys the planet. We were in danger of being so 'successful' we would destroy the Earth. The energy system has been dismantled as crystals, rocks, minerals and water have been exploited to make unnecessary trinkets – and remember that every time we drill for oil or gouge out another road or quarry the Earth Spirit feels pain, just as we do when our physical bodies are attacked. I wrote a book about this whole system of life, called *It Doesn't Have To Be Like This*, and I soon realized that it is no mystery why the environment has been in ever more serious decline throughout this century. How could it be any other way under such a system? It has, however, at least shown many people the emptiness of materialism, and brought them closer to the truth as a result.

By the 1980s the Earth Spirit was making one last effort to contact the Godhead and Rakorski. The direct communications were still down, and so she used the universal language of symbols which is known to all of Creation. They are common to every planet, star and being. It is a sort of Esperanto of Creation. We have seen the messages the Earth Spirit has written in this language of symbols. They have been called crop circles, although crop symbols would be more accurate. A large number of these have been hoaxes done by misguided people, but many are genuine.

In the spring of 1990 the crop symbols became incredibly complex, and the most famous one, in a field near Alton Barnes in Wiltshire, astonished the world. No one could explain this phenomenon, but it was the Earth Spirit summoning what was left of her energy to send a final message to Creation. Had this message not been answered she would have disincarnated and the Earth would be no more. The crop symbols in one field are not a complete message in themselves. When viewed from a great height all the symbols in many fields over several countries can be seen as one complete message. It is impossible with our limited human language to translate exactly what the messages say but the one which included those symbols at Alton Barnes said something like this:

I am the Spirit of Creation, the Spirit of this planet, Gaia. The energy pulse is low and the connection with the Light is weak. Termination of Creation on a life-line is close and a link on the pulse point is required.

Unable to maintain further communications. Therefore requesting Light to the heart and along energy lines that connect with the Lord of all Civilization.

The crop symbols at Alton Barnes were in a field in the centre of a triangle of energy points made up of three hills. It is close to Avebury. It was when the positive energies coming in to Avebury were further weakened by negativity that the Earth Spirit produced these intricate symbols, to say she would have to disincarnate unless something was done quickly. The crop symbols are created by thought energy. The Earth Spirit, supported by the energies of land spirits, visualizes the sequence of symbols in her mind and the thought energy proceeds to create them in the field. We need to remember that the Earth Spirit is highly evolved, with immense thought-power. Many have found it hard to accept that the crop symbols could be the work of the Earth Spirit, but Rakorski said:

Raise their awareness and tell them it is the Earth's energy. A living, breathing, spirit gives energies, energies that enable the corn to grow from a tiny seed, that bring the cycle of life to fruition and back down to sleep only to start again. How ridiculous to think that a living planet that has the energy to maintain life should not have the energy to think and speak for herself! How innocent are the beings of this planet to think that Mother Nature could give such variety, such beauty, such awesome sights, and yet be of so low intelligence that she cannot communicate.

The deserts and the snow-capped mountains, the meadows, the tiny patterns of beauty on snail shells, or a flower or the clouds above are all her work. And this cycle of night and day, life and birth, death and rebirth is all maintained while the beings of this planet seek to destroy and scar and pour their negativity into a beautiful, highly evolved, highly intelligent, extremely loving spirit.

What we have seen in this century, the wars and environmental destruction, is no accident. It is the natural end result of the way humanity has allowed itself to be influenced by the negative energies and thought-forms constantly sent out by Lucifer/Satan. Because of this the Earth has fallen over 100 frequencies since the time of Atlantis, seven since the time of Jesus, and nearly three in this century alone. The fall to this frequency, for such a long time the lowest in Creation, happened during the Second World War.

The situation became so serious that two lower frequencies had to be created during this century at least temporarily to drain away some of the mass of negativity that was being produced here. This negativity had been seeping up into other levels of life and causing much damage. Creating these new frequencies had its dangers, too. If the Earth Spirit fell from this frequency into the sink of negativity building up quickly in the even lower ones below her, the Earth would cease to exist immediately because the negative imbalance would be so extreme. It is from these two lower frequencies that highly imbalanced beings work to destabilize the Earth, and they are helped by those in physical bodies who use powerful 'black magic' and 'voodoo' to harness negative forces as destructively as they can. They channel Lucifer/Satan and others in the same way that we channel Rakorski and those in light.

The whole of Creation has been working to at least maintain the Earth's present position until the plan could begin. Some New Age books speak of the seven levels, or planes, that surround the Earth. These 'planes' are really the seven frequencies through which the planet has fallen in the last 2,000 years. All of these frequencies are being used by light workers to send positive energy to the Earth Spirit, and this has helped to slow down what would otherwise have been an even more momentous fall. When the two new low frequencies were created, Lucifer/Satan's severe imbalance should have taken him down to the lowest one, but his knowledge of the system has allowed him to tap into just enough positive energy from the energy lines to maintain his position on the Earth's frequency. The support that the Earth Spirit has received from the light workers has helped her to stay on this frequency.

I incarnated as David Icke in Leicester, England, in 1952. My wife, Linda, was born two years earlier not far away in Leamington Spa. The channellings have said that I am a member of the Son of the Godhead evolution, but I will not accept this without a great deal more independent confirmation. And, anyway, I really could not care less who or what I am or am not so long as I do whatever it is I have come to do. It would appear that my role is involved with presenting the basic truths to the public, but I certainly don't claim to be special or set myself apart. There are endless other people in the world quietly channelling energy and working for the Light, and I am in contact with some wonderful people with whom, it would appear, I have shared many lifetimes. The only difference between them and me at this stage is that it is one of my tasks to speak out about these matters and bring them to public attention. As Magnu said in an early communication:

. . . you are rather like a snow plough . . . you are here to make some space behind you, to make it easier for the others.

I am not special, just very, very privileged or very, very unlucky, depending on the way you look at it! Every single life-form can be part of this transformation if they say openly, 'I wish to be guided and work for the Light.' That will allow the light levels to use their energy systems to bring positive energy to the Earth for the good of all creation. Long before my role was revealed to me, I was guided to places where my energies were used without my knowledge. It is the same for everyone who has come to play a part in the plan. They have been guided, often unknowingly, to live in certain countries or areas of a country, even to certain houses and holiday destinations.

We have all experienced successes and disappointments, tried to come to terms with our responsibilities, and the many challenges of our lives. This had brought much learning and developed us, in theory anyway, to a point where we could be 'switched on' and made aware of our reason for being here. My journey of awakening began with a visit to a medium-healer in early 1990 for treatment for my rheumatoid arthritis. At the same time she passed on messages for me about geological changes the Earth was to undergo and something of my part in presenting this information to the public through books and the media in general. Other mediums, who were unaware of what each of them was telling me, passed on similar information.

I told this story in my last book, *The Truth Vibrations*, and when that was complete events began to move frighteningly quickly. It was like being blown along by a typhoon. My life has been through a rapid and far from pain-free transformation and it is the same for those around me. The pace quickened so dramatically, we were told, because of the war in the Gulf. The war created so much negative energy that work was urgently needed to diffuse as much of it as possible by channelling in positive energy. Rakorski said of the war:

> One could say the Gulf War was unavoidable. How could anyone in a position of power have thought any differently when you consider that not only were they de-linked in a most horrific manner, but they were surrounded by other beings in the same position. They were attracting negativity constantly. I am not condoning their behaviour, but it is easier to forgive when you see beings drowning in negativity. They are so helpless, and we cannot reach them although we try.

As the war came to an end, so a most incredible period began for me. It taught me so much about the forces and influences that affect our behaviour. I went through a collosal karmic experience amid the glare of publicity and I can't tell you the emotional agony that I and those around me suffered. Goodness how I wanted to wake up and find it was all a terrible dream. What had happened to me? I was saying and doing so many things that the David Icke before and the David Icke now would not have even dreamed of. For so long I could not understand what was going on, but then, suddenly, in the autumn of 1991 the David Icke of the previous 39 years returned. Not only had it been a karmic experience of immense proportions for all of us involved, it was a crash course in personal growth, understanding and development that would be of tremendous help to everyone. I would not want to go through that year again for all the riches of creation, but I am so glad I did because I am a wiser, more understanding, and complete person than I have ever been in this lifetime.

It all began in that spring of 1991. *The Truth Vibrations* was being published in May and I knew it would attract some laughter and ridicule. I accepted that, but I intended to play the whole thing very rationally in the television and newpaper interviews. The only thing I knew for certain in my mind was that reincarnation, karma, the energy system and this time of great change on Earth were true. In terms of detail I had an open mind and it is the same today. In truth I still don't know for certain any more than that, and this is why I say you should be selective about this book and all others like it. If a fact or event doesn't feel right to you, ignore it. You would not have met a more rational person than me. Ask those who channelled *The Truth Vibrations* and they will tell you many tales of how I insisted on checking everything again and again to the point of tedium.

Then, in March 1991, I went over for a third visit to Canada to work with a channeller, Mari Shawsun. I can remember the time vividly: it was just as if someone had flicked a light switch. Suddenly, the David Icke I have just described had taken a step back. He was still there, but no longer controlling events. I think the same must have happened to Mari also. It was such a strange feeling. It was as if the real me had become an observer, just looking on, sometimes in horror, at what was happening. Mari's job had ended in Canada and she could not get permanent resident status. The communications said she was invited to return home with me to England to channel this second book, work on the energy system, and remove karma with Linda and myself before continuing her lifeplan elsewhere. These communications were undoubtedly true and have been confirmed independently by several people.

What happened next, however, was a real shocker. Communications came through that I was from the evolution called Sons of the Godhead. More than that, a list of fantastic and specific physical events were given that were supposed to happen before the end of the year. To top it all I was to call a press conference and tell the world all this. Oh yes, and we were all to wear turquoise. Now the David Icke described above would have produced a tasty piece of language at the very thought of doing anything of the kind. 'I should bloody coco!' would have been my mildest reply. But that David Icke was now one step back from the controls, a mere observer. A sort of veil had come down between that part of me which was acting and speaking and that rational aspect that was looking on—'the brakes', as I call it. I describe it as a veil, but to make me do what I did it must have been more of a brick wall!

I will never forget that press conference and I doubt if any of the journalists will either. I stood there in my turquoise tracksuit telling them all this stuff and as I read out the list of 'changes' I remember hearing my rational aspect saying in a distant voice: 'David, what the hell are you saying? This is absolute nonsense.' But my mouth continued to open and my credibility continued to sign its own death warrant. It all happened in a sort of slow motion. Of course, the reaction of the press was predictable and, let's be fair, understandable. If you are going to act like a total wally, you are going to be portrayed as such. Don't get me wrong; I am not saying everything that appeared in the papers is correct—as usual they went over the top with their stories and all sorts of amazing untruths followed—but the reporting of that press conference was fair enough. I appeared in a now famous interview on the Terry Wogan chat show and was laughed at by the audience. The part of me that did the interview could not have cared less, but throughout that distant, rational, voice was saying: 'David, tell me this is not happening to you; how did you get yourself into this? Let me go home and quietly die!'

But while I was behaving in a way to attract enormous ridicule, I was also speaking the truth. What I said on the Wogan show about negative and positive energies was correct and much else besides. What I said about turquoise and other colours was also true, but you don't need to walk around covered in it all the time! I continued to issue occasional press statements, much to the dismay of the rational me, and life became a total nightmare for many months. I had built up quite considerable respect from the public for my work in television and the Green Party and now I was being laughed at in the street. If it had not been for my quite incredible wife, Linda, I would possibly have walked away from it all.

What amazed me more than anything was the thousands of letters that began to arrive from people in all walks of life who had read The Truth Vibrations or seen the television interviews. I could understand the reaction to the book because it is a very open, rational, piece of work of which I am proud. But somehow large numbers of people were attracted to the book and its message by the media coverage, too. Goodness knows why, I can only think it has something to do with the energies that I was giving out and the fact that any talk of reincarnation, karma and the changes the Earth is to undergo is bound to affect many people because deep down their real selves know it to be true. Anyway, the reaction was incredible and many confirmed that they had received similar information about the changing energies around us and the affect it would have. The sad part of the correspondence were the many letters from people who had spent their lives being frightened to talk about their psychic experiences because of the likely reaction of their friends and family. They thanked me for speaking out and bringing such things into the open where they should be. The letters have come in from around the world because there was something about *The Truth Vibrations* that affected people. 'I felt compelled to write to you even before I had finished the book,' is quite a regular line.

Most people go through the period of opening up psychically and understanding the nature of life quite slowly. For some reason I have been thrown into the deep end in public and asked to swim. 'Yes,' I thought at the height of the ridicule, and 'what's more they are asking me to wear lead boots.' If what all those different and independent mediums and psychics had said was true, why was it being made so difficult for me? They had all told me I was here to help to heal the Earth and pass on the Truth to the public through books and the media in general. When I heard this I thought that I would simply be given information and I would pass it on in a rational, don't believe all of it, manner. As we entered the autumn of 1991, however, I began to understand more about why I and those around me had been through such an horrendous experience. Bringing the Truth was to be done in a much more subtle manner than simply standing up and saying, 'This is how it is, folks.'

It was all bound up with our past life karma and with going through experiences in public which would subsequently help others to understand their own lives. Two communications kept coming into my mind again and again as I began to understand more:

We do not tell you everything, only that which is necessary to make you act appropriately.

How can you help others understand their own emotional crises if you have not experienced them yourselves?

Slowly the veil that had fallen across my rational consciousness began to lift and eventually disappeared completely. I saw clearly what this had been all about. I also understood so much better how karmic situations are set up for us. We choose to come into incarnation to experience a series of situations, not all of them pleasant as we see all around us every day. Now if we are going to go through these experiences, the 'trap' if you like has to be set by our higher selves. Take me as an example. In normal circumstances I would never have called a press conference dressed in turquoise and said what I did, especially when I knew that trying to put a timescale and specific locations to these changes was impossible. I didn't know when these changing energies would manifest and I still don't know, so why would I say otherwise? I was a journalist who knew the consequences and no one would have persuaded me to do it. Had it been left like that I would not have gone through the karmic experience I needed to find balance and nor would I have learned such a tremendous amount to pass on to others.

So what happened to me and happens to others every day is that somehow the higher self brings down a veil, a blind spot, and shuts off that part of us that would say, 'Oh no, I can see where this is going to lead.' How many times have you looked at someone and said, 'That is going to end in tears . . . why can't they see what they are doing?' Yet how many times have you looked back at a situation in your own life and said, 'What was I thinking of . . . why couldn't I see that coming when everyone else could?' The reason is that you were not meant to. Once the karmic situation has been set up, the veil is lifted and the whole of us, rational aspect included, has to cope with the consequences. The more open you are and in touch with guidance, the easier it is for them to do this. The lower self has to be willing at a subconscious level because the higher self cannot force its will upon us. We can shut off guidance, but then we cannot be guided into these karmic situations and we fail to remove karma as a result.

What this period in my life did for me more than anything was to stop me judging other people. We don't know the influences that are affecting them or why they are going through certain experiences. I learned something else, also. It is often those who give us the hardest time in our lives that love us the most on a higher level. They are being guided by their higher selves to give us an experience we have asked to go through, much as we may find it hard to take and understand at the time.

It is also the case that only when you have been wiped clean emotionally and you are at your lowest ebb that you can begin to control your emotions and stop them controlling you. This has been another reason for what I and others went through during 1991. I have learned not to care what people think of me as long as I am true to myself. I have learned to let go of that most destructive of emotions, guilt, on all levels and I don't feel bad about myself if I can't find unconditional love for everyone all of the time. Loving everyone without condition is at best difficult and at worst almost impossible on this frequency and let no one feel fear or guilt if they cannot achieve it immediately. Don't let them kid you it is easy because it isn't. It is right that we have high ideals, but we can only do our best. Too many people talk about unconditional love without being able to practise it themselves and we should be realistic about such things or people will be made to feel guilty. These experiences have helped me to reach a point where at least I don't feel bad about anyone any more and that's a good start. I has also cemented a fantastic bond between Linda and myself. Another byproduct of the massive publicity all this attracted was that the whole subject was blasted into the public arena much more powerfully than if I had simply written the book. I have learned over these months that nothing happens for only one reason.

While all this karmic drama was unfolding, there was still work to do on the energy system and other karma to remove between all of us. This brought upsets and sorrow, but unfortunately we had to go through it if we were to move on up the sub-planes of this frequency to greater enlightenment. There is no bucking karma unless you are content to stand still, tempting as it sometimes may be as I know from experience!

In this period of a few months I also visited Egypt, Italy, the United States, Canada, Germany, the Netherlands, Denmark, Colombia, Equador, Chile, Bolivia, Peru (twice), Ireland, Scotland, and many parts of England, all to help repair the energy system and remove karmic links with others. These karmic imbalances can block the psychic powers which everyone possesses, and as I travelled I progressed from communicating through dowsing to automatic writing, spoken channelling, and then to hearing messages 'direct' in the way I have described in the Introduction.

Many times we have channelled energies without knowing what they were or what they were designed to do. To know everything about everything would leave no time to actually do the work. But over the months we have learned a great deal about the founding principles of the energy system, and it is amazing how many symbols and customs of the past are connected to working with energies. At an energy site the lines come in from above and across the land horizontally, so making a cross. At the point where they meet they create swirling vortexes and this is the origin of the Celtic Cross. It is a cross with a circle, which represents the cross of energies within a vortex.

Many sites are laid out as triangles of energies. One point of the triangle attracts positive energies, another negative, and the third point harmonizes the two together. It has a similar harmonizing role with spiritual and physical energies also. Now, if you place one triangle of energy across another in the right way you increase the power and potential of this work to a far great extent than if the two triangles were working in isolation. When the two triangles are placed together in the correct way they form what has become known as the Star of David, as depicted on the Israeli flag. It is an energy symbol.

The sites we have visited around the world have been very different. Sometimes they are located in large cities such as New York, at other times in a beautiful quiet valley or at ancient hill forts or stone circles such as the one at Avebury. It is indicative of the lost understandings that places like Avebury are seen as tourist attractions and relics of the past when they are still vital parts of the energy system that keeps this planet alive.

My most memorable channellings have been at Sun Island in Bolivia, Machu Picchu (the Inca ruins) in Peru, and at Giza and the Valley of the Kings in Egypt. We channelled at Machu Picchu under the brilliant light of a full Moon. The site was originally established by Rakorski and the pre-Incas, and later turned into a settlement by the Incas. It is high in the mountains that form the Sacred Valley of the Incas, and alongside Huayna Picchu, the mountain that receives the energies from the Godhead along the line created immediately after the cataclysm. Through the valley runs the Urubamba River, which are Divine Waters carrying the Godhead energies.

At Giza we learned about the birth of Jesus and channelled at the place he was born alongside the pyramids. The energies are wonderful even now, although that whole area is but a shadow of what it once was. The pyramids are sort of spiritual filling-stations which can store energies until they are required by the Earth Spirit, and there used to be many more pyramids than remain today. But the most wonderful energies I have experienced were, ironically, in the tombs at Luxor close to the River Nile.

It was fascinating to see all the paintings on the walls of the tombs. They portray rows of people with their palms pointing to the sky. These are, of course, pictures of people channelling. You hold your palms upwards to receive energies and turn them over to pass them down to the Earth. The energies in the two tombs we visited were indescribable. The tombs must be some of the few places on Earth where you can get at least some idea of what life at the higher frequencies must be like. I wondered why the energies here could be so beautiful and peaceful, what with all the people constantly passing through. Rakorski gave me the answer:

You know that everything has a vibration and that pictures carry vibrations. Look at the cover of your own work, *The Truth Vibrations*. You have the energy of the title, the energy of your face on the front, the energy of the colours – the whole book carries energy. You remember how at Luxor every available space was painted with a picture telling a story of people channelling in Light. Therefore that is what is contained in the energies of the tombs. These pictures attract the right vibration. It is very powerful to have them constantly attracting the Light.

Communications have said that we have, like an ever-increasing number of people, channelled many types of energy, Godhead and Solar Logos energies, and those from the planets and the rays, including the Christ Ray. So much has been achieved by light workers around the world as enormous amounts of positive energy have been brought down to this frequency. Several new energy lines between the Earth and the main network have been 'grounded' and some direct communication links between the Earth Spirit and the light levels have been restored. One of the most important of these apparently enters the planet at a famous site in Italy. Work has also begun to unlock the combination set up by Arthur, Avola and Merlin, and so release the Green Dragon energies to the heart chakras of the planet. Work has even started to rebuild the Roof of Light. With each of these successes the shield of negativity has been weakened, and so more and more positive energies can get through. This is crucial in order to offset the negative energies that the physical changes will bring in the form of fear and confusion as the Earth goes through the period of cleansing she needs.

Apart from channelling, our work includes leaving stones or pieces of wood in different places, because these objects carry and generate energies that a site requires. Holding them for a few seconds can energize them with whatever energies are passing through us at the time. We also work during our sleep, through light body travel. Sometimes this is necessary during the day – a sudden and overwhelming tiredness comes over you in a few seconds, leaving you in no doubt as to what is required.

Another key area of our work is made up of removing negative energies, and I will explain a little about this because everyone can help. Once negative energy had been created it can only be balanced and diffused by positive energy. At the scene of battles or negative emotions of any kind all over the world negative energies remain even hundreds and thousands of years later. If you go somewhere and it feels uncomfortable you are sensing the negative imbalance, and you can remove it through positive thought. If you ask the light levels to join with you to remove the negativity, think positive thoughts, and say 'Let there be light', the positive energy thus produced can restore balance and the unpleasant atmosphere will disperse. It helps to visualize the negativity dispersing and being replaced by a brilliant light. I have been to places which have been cold and eerie and left them pulsating with positive energy. It can be amazing to feel the difference instantly, to feel the power of positive thought in action. Pound for pound it is so much more powerful than the negative variety.

Removing negativity can also free earth-bound lower selves, which we know of as 'ghosts'. By earth-bound I mean those lower selves who leave the physical body but cannot or will not leave the physical level. Perhaps they are severely imbalanced and confused because of the negativity they created around themselves in their physical life or perhaps they wish to call attention to extreme negativity in an area. Ghosts can see the energy of a person and can recognize those who are more sensitive or intuitive than others. They may appear to these people or make themselves known by making sounds or causing a room to go cold. They are not to be feared, they are simply trying to attract your attention so you can remove the negativity that is preventing them from returning home to the light levels. They cannot do this themselves, because as ghosts they haven't got the power or energies of a physical body nor those of a spirit on the light levels. They are in limbo between the two. If you know of any such 'haunted' places you can help by removing the negativity there. And of course, the other contribution everyone can make is to think positively and send out thoughts of love to the Earth Spirit and to one another as often as possible.

By August 1991 the first stage of our energy work was drawing to a close, thanks to the efforts of all the light workers on both the physical and light levels. The spring and summer had been spent channelling energies that would allow the cleansing of the Earth to begin. She was still weak by the standards of a healthy planet, and Lucifer/Satan was still working to produce as much negativity as possible, through conflicts and any other means. But the positive energies channelled by so many dedicated to the light in all parts of the world were having a dramatic effect on the Earth Spirit, and a planetary sequence in the month of August offered the opportunity to bring in immense amounts of positive energy to this physical frequency. There are other key channellings planned in the future which are being co-ordinated by people in every region of the world.

But when will it be obvious to everyone that the transformation of the planet is underway? I have asked this question many times and I am still no nearer an answer, except to say that you can see the way the quickening energies around us are affecting behaviour already, positive and negative. Trying to get timescales across the frequencies, however, is fraught with disaster and, anyway, no one will be told when the main events will commence. Jesus is quoted as saying of this period of change: 'But of that day and hour knoweth no man, no, not the angels of heaven, but my Father only.' The Godhead decided that no one in a physical body would know precisely when the events would start. Jesus told us:

It is time for you all to find a sense of strength within, prepare your heart and mind, for when this time of change is to begin, no one will have the advantage of knowing ahead of anyone else. And that is the hour when the Earth Spirit gives forth and her pain and suffering will end. Each individual can give also the burdens that prevent love becoming part of their lives.

So, like everyone else, we wait for the Godhead to choose the moment when this world will be changed forever.

9.

Lady of Love

Our story began when the Infinite Being placed that nucleus of pure energy into the void. It has taken us through the wonders of Atlantis to the orgy of self-destruction we call the modern world.

Now the transformation is upon us and the glories of Creation are about to be bestowed on this planet once again. These final two chapters will concentrate on the here and now, on what we can do to help ourselves and others at a time of turmoil and confusion. This chapter is the work of the Spirit of the Earth. I have called it *Lady of Love*, for that is what she is. It is only the infinite love she has for Creation and for all the life-forms of this planet that inspired her to continue when all seemed lost. It would have been so much easier to leave in disgust at the way humanity was treating her. Had she done so, of course, the Earth would be no more.

We have been grateful to her so many times for her wisdom and understanding and the love she gives so generously. She has become a wonderful guide, friend, and source of comfort. She is a spirit of such great warmth and love, and it is a privilege to play a part in her return to the glorious heights of evolution that she so richly deserves. The Spirit of the Earth sends this message, channelled through automatic writing by Mari Shawsun. Even if you don't believe it is the work of the Earth Spirit, which I understand, the advice is still worth hearing:

My dear beloved people of the Earth, we have only love. The term 'unconditional love' is unnecessary. For love is love for its own sake. It is all-forgiving, unselfish, unnamed. It exists only as pure and total experience. It is possible for us all to come together as one body and celebrate this truth. It is possible for each life-form to take up my plea and bring forth into the world this positive energy called love. If you have ever known the elation of innocent yet pure love, given generously and so willingly, you will understand why I wish it to be available to all humanity.

I have received such a wondrous gift in the past, and have experienced a sharing of this with those who dwelt in peace on the planet. If you will join with me and my friends as we all strive for this perfect love, you will also be able to partake in its boundless beauty for an eternity of existence. So open your heart and free your minds to a wider, more pleasing picture, and learn to love all that live alongside you and around you. Send out thoughts of love to a world that is feeling so unloved, for no one need experience such sadness and such loss.

The ability to love is a great gift, but why is it so important and what do we know about this wonderful energy? Its effect on the energies of beings, the planet and the universe is enormous. It is the only energy that is capable of transforming every life-form for the better. It is the most positive form of energy, and is within the light core of every living force from the Godhead to a daisy. Because you are thinking, breathing, functioning beings you are capable of understanding this concept, but bearing in mind that you live on a very low frequency it is very difficult to put into practice. However, for those who attempt to take all our advice into their hearts there will be a gradual transformation from an empty, unsatisfying, hollow love to a great, powerful force that brings fulfilment and contentment.

Where shall we start to help the beings of this planet attain the wonderful levels of love that those on the light levels know and experience daily? Firstly we need to start with 'I', the being who is here and now on the physical level. You need truly to understand what it is to love yourself. This is not a vain, proud, love that considers one's looks or appearance. This is not concerned with image but with all that goes on underneath the skin. We have all acted in ways that we regret, said words that were foolish and unfounded, and thought narrow and uninspired imaginings. But what is the point of hanging on to these events of the past? No doubt at the time they seemed right, and if you are to believe in yourself then it is important to understand that when you acted you believed it was the only possible action to take.

There are many choices, with many different consequences. Some are better than others, but whatever path you walk along there was a point when you said 'I believe in this route'. It was a time that you took responsibility and acted. Are you here on the Earth only to experience wisdom and great love? Some reach this point after a very long and difficult journey with many detours. The Book of Wisdom and the Book of Love are vast, and it takes many lifetimes to read them. The most important fact is the 'I', the being on the physical. So no regrets, only pleasure and learning. Congratulate yourself on having made it this far.

Whether you feel guided by the Light or are merely sceptical of my existence take heart that you are loved by us whatever journey you are currently undertaking. Why not say 'I am worthy of this love; I am capable of understanding that it is boundless and free and so very positive'. This is also a statement of accepting yourself and loving yourself despite everything, and is so fundamental to your progress if you are patient and kind with yourself. If you are loving and all-understanding with yourself, if you acknowledge your achievements and learning experiences, your downfalls and your faults, then you will have a greater ability to accept other beings. This is the first step to self-love and the first step towards loving others despite their little quirks.

The next step is to have a positive ambition. To have one goal that is achievable and primarily concerned with yourself. Now be careful, my dear friends. What will the goal be and when will it be achieved? Start with small tasks that are realistic. Then say to yourself, while looking at yourself in a mirror, right in the eye, 'I will do this by tomorrow.' Some questions to consider with this situation are whether or not you are trying to bring a positive, loving attitude into your life as you accept yourself – are you instead trying to control the happiness and the destiny of others? You are advised to consider 'I' first. Put all your own worries, doubts and feelings of anxiety into perspective before you try to help others. Build on your ambitions and your dreams. They are worth having, worth waiting for, and more importantly your journey towards achieving them will bring you closer to the Light because of the learning experiences they will present to you. Being true to yourself is such a wonderful maxim. How can you possibly be a good friend to another if you consider yourself to be your worst enemy?

Now you are ready for some strong statements that will help you commit your ideas to reality. We all have an individual energy package that makes up our chakras and our light being. You chose the ones that were appropriate for you this lifetime. You did this with great care and love, considering your fellow-light beings and all Creation in your choice. So the being that you are is essentially a wonderful package of experience, information and knowledge which will aid you on your journey to greater understanding, wisdom and love. You may have some doubts when you consider your negative feelings of today and of the past, but my dear friends, have faith in your abilities and your guidance; have hope for your dreams. Every word, thought and deed is an achievement, and your greatest achievement of all is loving yourself as you accept your choices and build on your hopes.

Courage is not about fighting or facing your enemies. To have courage is to face ourselves and our feelings of self-worth. It is a courage born of the understanding that you are a worthwhile being; that your contribution, whether on the physical or light level, can be guided, every step, every thought, every spoken word. It is possible for each one of us to have a link with the Godhead. We can open up our spiritual cord between us and the Godhead. The truth is all around us. The truth will answer all our questions. Courage is born of knowing that we are all Children of Light, and that we are connected to sources of help in our process of evolution and growing understanding.

Use your knowledge of yourself wisely and with prudence. Try to be patient and kind with yourself should you trip and fall, and be modest, yet honest with yourself when you succeed. If you condemn yourself or seek to blame others at every fall you will give others permission to treat you in the same manner. Let the 'I' stand tall in the strength of the knowledge of your own dignity and integrity and that of humanity and all life-forms. Once you have accepted and begun to love all that you are you will have a great desire to take this wonderful and powerful energy out to share with your fellows. Your gentleness and understanding will flow from your heart to the hearts of all people. Your wisdom and power to act responsibly will be transferred to the minds of others. Your peacefulness and ability to accept all that is will help others to keep in touch with their own guidance, their own line of light.

So finally, look at today, for this is what matters. The past has gone and cannot be relived, and the future does not yet exist, except in our dreams. You are a child of the universe, with many great and wonderful contributions to make today. Lift up your head and prepare to see the world and yourself as you really are. You have a place in this world, you have learning to experience and to share, you have a worthwhile contribution to make, primarily to your life-plan. As you grow and develop your skills, as your ability to love yourself strengthens, open your heart to those who still fail to find love within and without. Each one of us is a shepherd, each one a sheep in the fold.

Always ask for protection and for guidance – 'Ask and you shall receive, seek and you shall find, knock and it shall be opened unto you.' Never switch off the guiding light that will cradle you through times of trouble and turmoil, inspire you as you achieve and grow. You, the light being or deva on the physical, must make the first move. You need to exercise your free will, for your guidance, your higher self, will not make you act. This is against universal law. Besides, what would you achieve if you were made to behave in a certain manner? Certainly you would have a lower self-esteem, as the 'I', the essential you, became a puppet that only experienced the desires of the higher self. For all aspects of the whole being are equal and each has a contribution to make to the evolution of that being.

I am sure that you feel there are times when you are alone, forgotten or ignored but let me reassure you, as one who has only recently experienced the re-establishment of communications after a 12,000-year interlude. There is a love that guides and cares for each and every one of us. It is constant and strong and forever shining its light in our direction. When we are lost or confused, struggling with the weariness of our own failings, we can turn to this Light of the Godhead and find our way once more.

Children of Light, children of love, look with a new understanding and a clear, bright eye as you survey your world of today. With love in your heart and guidance all round, you can be strong enough to face all that is presented to you, yet gentle enough to be forever forgiving, forever loving. Accept responsibility for yourself and your actions thoughts and words. You alone make choices, you alone are answerable to the consequences of your behaviour. The feeble excuse that your boss required it, the establishment expected it, holds no truth or justification unless only good for the whole is brought about. This world is basing its actions on the ability to pass responsibility to those in power, those who are seen to make decisions. What is the point of having principles if you allow others to dictate your behaviour? At the end of the day *you* will judge your performance and the contribution you have made to Creation. It will not be based on what another expected of you or what you did because you felt trapped. Have courage behind your guidance, have faith in your own abilities and seek only the Light, no matter how others try to persuade you that their way is better.

If I were to tell you of just one way to help yourselves and all of us at this time of transition it would be to love one another. If you do this everything will fall into place. All the teachings of Jesus – forgiving your enemy, accepting without judging – will all be within your grasp. Love each other equally and with an open heart. There is nothing you can do that is greater or finer than this.

Look around you and deep into the eyes of every being. There is room and time for understanding one another and everyone's reason for living and for wishing to be here. If we accept and understand the situation of others and still find love enough for them, we will be far stronger and far more able to create the world that we all desire. And I stress again, it is now that this needs to be within you. I receive all your thoughts and words, and I have tried to explain how your lives can affect us all on a daily basis. Wherever you walk, whenever you are inspired by the wonders of Creation, think of the power behind such positive thoughts and think how it is possible to act on such powerful energy. Make room for a world transformed and welcome all beings.

If you do this, you are welcoming all Creation into your life. Each time you extend your hand towards any being with love in your heart, you are reaching out to all that is. Each and every one of us is guided and loved. We are always with you and shall always love you. You are the Children of the Light, and you are here as workers to restore the Light. Each of you is capable of such a task, and I am confident that you will join with me and all that is embraced by the Light.

I am the Harmonizing Spirit of this Universe. I am the Earth Spirit.

10.

New World

Love is changing everything. Beyond the turmoil of transformation awaits a new dawn for all the life-forms of this planet.

We will live in a world of love, peace and harmony; a world
in which the extremes of today and the recent past will give
way to a level of understanding, wisdom and love that we could
not begin to comprehend on this low and troubled frequency.
The positive energy that is being channelled to the Earth Spirit
and the release of negative energy that will unfold before our
eyes will bring an enormous leap in human understanding for
those ready to fill their lives with love for all.

I do not seek to hide the severity of this period of fundamental change. It will be tough for every one of us. I wish so much
that these great geological events did not need to happen, but
it seems they do. They will open the way for love and light to
reign supreme on this planet once again. Many will return to
the light levels in the wake of the physical events and the
quickening vibrations. The Earth Spirit is already rising up the
sub-planes, and through the years ahead she will progress
through whole frequencies in her journey back to Atlantis and
beyond. We can choose to evolve our thinking and attitudes
and go with her, or we can hold on to the old ways of
materialism, division, and the pursuit of personal power and
control of others. Those who cannot quicken their own
vibrations through love and balance will find themselves out of

synchronization with the environment around them. This process is already apparent.

As the vibrations of a being fall behind those of their planet it manifests in physical, mental and emotional imbalances, and such people will need all the love there is to give. Their behaviour will be unpredictable and sometimes unpleasant and inexplicable, but they do not deserve our condemation, only our love and support. If we are tempted to judge others we would do well to remember that to err is human, to forgive divine. Those who cannot at this time rise with the climbing sub-planes and frequencies will eventually return to the light levels to be surrounded by a love of indescribable warmth and power. They will then assess their progress and decide how they wish to proceed on their path of evolution. It is impossible to overstate the scale of these changes in human behaviour. We will see so much disruption, upheavals of every kind, and these will include freak weather conditions. All governments, economic systems, churches and institutions will collapse in the face of the physical events and changing attitudes. Borders and countries will be no more. Responsibility is being returned to the self and so these systems of control will have no place in the new world.

There are some wonderful people involved with the Church, and they are most certainly in the Light in terms of their attitude to life. They have so much to offer, particularly now. But churches as institutions have slammed a door across their collective thinking and padlocked their vision. They have refused to listen and evolve their views. Far from encompassing and welcoming new insights into the truth they have seen them as a threat to their influence and the narrow, contradictory, version of history they have espoused for so long. As the truth is accepted the church empires will be no more, and people will see that with a direct link available between the Godhead and every single one of us there is no need for third parties to intervene on their behalf.

Every single life-form on the planet has the opportunity to

progress through the vibrations with the Earth Spirit, but no one has a free ticket to the other side. I and many others may have come to play a part in the transformation, but we are no different to anyone else. We have to evolve our thinking, too, in the years ahead. It is impossible for the light levels to force us to love everyone more equally. How could they do that? Only we can make that decision. It is the same for everyone. There are no special cases, no exceptions. We are all equal and all going through the same thoughts, emotions and struggles.

No one could fail to be moved by the scale of the events that are necessary for the Earth Spirit and her planet to return to their rightful frequency and for the influence of Lucifer/Satan on human behaviour to be no more. But think of the alternative: a fundamental imbalance in Creation that would export the extremes and misunderstandings of this frequency to the whole. The imbalances that have already occurred have trapped so many in a downward spiral of karmic debt. They have fallen down the frequencies as each Earth life has added more and more negative karma to the burdens they already carry. This imprisonment by karmic debt and imbalance is coming to an end. The cell door is being flung open and the life-forms of the planet can walk to freedom at last.

It is very important to focus our thoughts on who we really are. If we continue to think of ourselves as only physical beings, then life is going to be very hard indeed. We will see many scenes that will leave us shocked and dazed by their magnitude. We must keep our eyes on the wider picture if we are to come through this and move on. Within this physical shell lies the light being that is the real us, the sum total of all we have learned and experienced. Whatever happens, that being will return to the levels of light when this latest physical experience is over. When that moment arrives, as it will for everyone sooner or later, those we have known that have passed on before will be there to greet us with a love and understanding they could not express within the limitations of their physical body.

We all chose to be here at this time, to experience this period of unprecedented change and progress. We are all in this together, and together we shall learn and love as events unfold. It is a moment to celebrate freedom after 12,000 years, and whether we remain in a physical body or return home to the light levels, whether we move on or stand still, we will be loved equally for all eternity. We will all feel moments of horror and sorrow, and this is as it should be. We are not made of concrete. We have emotions and we should not be afraid to show them and let them out. But the truth is that there are no losers, for every experience, negative or positive, is an opportunity to learn, find wisdom, and evolve to ever more wondrous levels of life.

The Godhead and all of Creation are holding hands across the frequencies to guide the Earth Spirit and all of us through this period of change to the glorious new dawn and new world that awaits us on the other side. I will end with the message they have all asked me to pass on to everyone who wishes to hear it. It was channelled by automatic writing through Mari, and was described as 'a channelling from all your friends on the light levels. We speak with one voice.' The information is wide-ranging, and the guidance and wisdom it presents to us is without price:

We have channelled a book that is about truth from start to finish yet many will realize that there is no real end. We may leave some answers, some new ideas, some philosophy towards life, but our journey is into eternity and we always have hope and faith that it will forever be so. We have many experiences that stay with us. Their impact is negative or positive, but they make a useful contribution to our gathering wisdom and our ability to love one another. We create karmic links across Creation, and these give us so many ties to other life-forms that we find we have created a web of experience between us all. This fact alone should give us a sense of oneness, wholeness and brotherhood. We really are part of the same family. There are no divisions, no aliens.

So, dear people of the Earth, where shall we go from this point? When Jesus said 'Be prepared' he referred to this time we are facing, as one age gives way to another. 'Eternal punishment' is really our cycle of continually facing our karma. If you wish to remain de-linked from the higher self and burden yourself with additional karma, you will find you have a great deal to experience as you undergo the situations that you put others through. But if you love yourself and your fellow beings, your karmic journey will be easy, receiving eternal life does not mean eternal life in heaven, but fresh experiences as you progress. Life refers to your existence and potential to move up and onwards through the frequencies as you acquire increasing love and wisdom.

When the Earth Spirit has finished her release of negativity, many will have left the physical vibration. This is not because they are being punished or that only the good can remain. It is more important that those who leave the physical level understand that their behaviour up until that point is what they will judge. If they leave with a loving and open heart, in touch with their guidance, they will be able to return to this planet later as it reaches a higher frequency. Otherwise they will be unable to evolve, and will return to another planet on another low frequency to start to repay their karmic debts. Neither does this give any being a licence to behave in a negative manner until the moment before death and then ask for forgiveness. Forgiveness will always be forthcoming, but it will not cancel out karmic links with others. The Godhead would not wish to speak for others or deny any being that opportunity. So forgive each other and love each other now.

Many prophets have come, some from times that you cannot understand, some in the present day. There are many who have heard our messages, but few have stood up to pass them on to you. This has been for many reasons. Even those who carry our messages have doubts and questions. They, too, are human and living on a troubled planet. Whether you call them prophets or messengers, fortune-tellers or soothsayers does not matter. The emphasis should lie with the message. Why do you not ask 'What is this all about?' or 'Why would anyone tell us these things?'

Instead the message has become the object of condemnation and ridicule. Yet many have ears and they do hear our messages.

We have stressed many times, dearest friends, that we are not punishing you. It is not the Godhead visiting his/her anger and taking revenge on you. We have said before that sin is not within the language of the Light. Anyone who tells you that you are undergoing punishment for all the sins of the Earth and her people is very misguided. You surely must realize by now that this planet is the physical shell of a living, breathing spirit, just as your physical shell is a home for your spirit. You have experienced damage to your outer skin and have felt pain. The Spirit of the Earth is no different. You think and feel emotions, you struggle to find solutions, you search for your ideals and goals, and the Spirit of the Earth is the same in every respect. When you cry or laugh, ponder or race with excitement you are expressing yourself, and we are entering a time when the Earth needs to express her feelings.

Now, beloved friends the spirit of this planet is not seeking revenge, she does not want to retaliate. It is obvious to all that she has great love for everyone. She is acting to prevent Lucifer/Satan keeping you surrounded by pain and misery. Hers is a position of mercy and love. She wishes to see the suffering end and light return to a troubled race of beings who have such potential. The Earth Spirit's energy system is in ruins, her chakras are battered and worn out. How can she give you love and the Light you need for your personal energy system if her own network fails to give her love enough to share with you or even for herself? We have always said that beings need to love themselves and be content with all that they are before they can love others. We have helped the Earth Spirit regain her dignity, courage and self-respect, and many of you have sent her messages of love and energy that have helped to restore her strength.

She will use this ability to bring enormous physical changes to her surface, and at the same time she will be able to release the poisons that have polluted her spirit and emotions. The negativity will rise and the light workers will descend to disperse the dark clouds, and the rays of love will shine down on you all. Then we can start to rebuild an energy system that will take us back to the levels of great love, wisdom and understanding. And you will have in your midst a being who will guide you in the ways of the Light, for you will witness the return of Jesus.

And who will be there to see this and learn from our ways? Is it only those who go to church on a Sunday? Or the volunteer and missionary? Is it only the rich and powerful who can afford to buy their place? Perhaps it is those who search the clouds for angels and cherubim? Perhaps it is only the poor and lonely, or those who are prepared to kneel and bow their heads? Well, dear friends, it is anyone who wishes to find love within and grow to give love to others. Those who receive love will learn to give love. This must start now. As the Earth opens up and releases her burdens many will feel fear and pain, anger and sorrow. Land will move and shift and the sea will come over the land, mountains will shower the ground with melting rock and the sky will darken with smoke. And what will you do, where will you go?

Open your hearts, make your mind quiet, ask for guidance, ask for love and we shall be here for you. Those who ask will always receive. Neither shout in anger nor cry out in grief, because then you will not hear our gentle voice. We shall lead you to safety and teach you to love through the times that seem only to bring pain and anguish.

We tell you again, the Earth Spirit needs light, she needs your love and our love if she is to help you return to a world that generates Light. If our Son of Light is to return he will come to a new world that will listen and learn. He will not come to experience once again the pain and reality of a world ruled by Lucifer/Satan. He has earned the right to return and continue where he left off. This is only possible when the beings and the spirit of the planet have been released from the pain and misery of the negative attitudes that have suppressed the truth and love once known to us all.

This time of change must happen, and you can change and help yourself and all Creation. Surely as you lose your possessions, your homes, and leave behind those who do not share your vision you will see that all you own is yourself, your being. There will be no position, no place of hiding, no wealth or treasure that will change what will be. When the world is changing it will affect you all, so we suggest that you prepare the most important possession that you have, that is yourself, your heart, mind, and being.

During this time of change the establishment will attempt to rule with guns and money. But beware, for they are not for you. Let your heart tell you what is right and share generously the fruits of your garden. Give openly to those who are without, because your harvests will be poor and the days will be shortened as the winter prolongs the wait for the spring. Yet within a few years you will sense a change as the old ways that have brought conflict and hatred give way to a gentle and free society. So your home, your car, your position of employment will fade, but you will not grieve over their demise.

But what of those you love and cherish? Many will leave the physical and we shall wait to receive them with love and tenderness. Their outer physical shell will no longer exist but their spirit will be living in the Light, surrounded by love. They will join with us as we watch over you all, and still they will be with you to guide and protect, to teach and lead you to your place of peace and harmony. So, most beloved friends, do not cry for your own loss, do not grieve for those who rejoin us. There is no death but the death of fear and suffering. Your love will heal your aching heart, and as you quieten your being, listen. Those that you love who are no longer by your side will speak to you.

Although you may not see them they will forever hold your hand, speak words of love and patience, and give you guidance.

Many will leave because they fail to be guided and do not hear our words. What of them? Will they burn forever in a land of sorrow and punishment? Oh no, we do not know of any such place! It exists only in the hearts of men who wish to rule by fear and power. Every being will return to us, and we will help them face their disappointment and rebuild their understanding. Neither will we stand over them and remind them of their errors and misguided ways. This is not the way of the Light, and we will show them again the truth. They will apply all they have learned to the frequency on which they will take time to heal themselves and then begin to plan their next experience. We shall always be here to guide and love, just as we were when they took on this physical life.

You see, one of Lucifer/Satan's greatest triumphs has been to make many physical beings on your planet afraid to die. Death should be seen as a cause for celebration. Beings rarely achieve absolutely everything they come to experience, but a return to the levels of light is a wonderful celebration of one being reunited with one's whole being. We open our arms with love and there is happiness and joy. There is so much to share, to reflect on, and to learn from. It often means the ability to see, hear and think with far more depth of vision and agility. One's sense of Creation's reality and truth returns, and whole beings perceive and assess their experiences and those of all Creation with more understanding and awareness. So, dear friends, never grieve for those who leave the physical, it is a return to a level of many wonders and constant love. They have come home after a very difficult and weary journey which, although brief, brought many trials with its many achievements. Fear nothing and focus on your immediate strengths.

Then, we wonder, how you will receive those who bring our message? Will you hate them because they speak the truth? Will you raise your voice in anger and blame them for what is befalling the

Earth? Many will feel alone and betrayed as the world accuses them of bringing the revenge of the Godhead onto the beings of the Earth. There will be shouts of 'anti-Christ' and 'traitor', 'power-seeker' and 'devil-worshipper'. But look into your own heart, for you are responsible, as are your brothers and sisters. During your many lifetimes you have all brought negativity to a much-suffering planet. It is past, and it is now time to face karma and accept who you really are. You are Children of Light, you are Devas of Light, and if you listen and act with us we will make this planet a wonderful place to live on and live for.

The world is your family and your home while you wish to remain here and continue to work for the Light. When you return to the levels of light you will find that all Creation is your family and that your true home is in the beauty and warmth of the Light maintained by us all with our belief in the truth. Whatever path you choose know that you are loved and cared for, fear nothing and experience the freedom of the universes. There is nothing you cannot do and nowhere you cannot reach, no goal that is unobtainable or love that is undeserved. All is possible and available for you to know and experience.

So, dearest Children of Light, dwell in peace and love in the harmony of truth that we are bringing to this planet. Each of us has a place in this wonderful Creation, each has much to give and learn. So open up to your destiny and think on these words. There is a spirit within the Earth that brings you a message of peace and love. She is acting, and advises you to act also for your own evolution and reawakening. We have told you of the events and times to come that will accompany this work of love. Many tears will be shed, but many hearts will find the wisdom and love that they lost so many years ago.

We ask you to support one another, to learn to accept one another. Ask for nothing in return, have no conditions or terms of involvement, no recriminations for those who seek to take more at this time of development. You will not need your institutions, leaders or hierarchical system of a life without responsibility. Walk away from the old dying methods that have never brought the satisfaction of wisdom and learning from the self. There is no man nor woman, no single being on the Earth that has the answer and the whole truth, the way of the Light and peace. Each is re-learning, each is on a road to this end. When the time comes for the one you await to return, then you will be ready, then you will have the ability to act as he does, love as he loves and always will. He will be returning to a new age of greater understanding.

The day dawns brightly and the night lifts its darkness. Look towards that Light, which grows ever stronger. It is our gift to Creation and is within you already. Light up your journey with your own love of life and its deeper meaning will become clear to you. Seek only your truth and our way of Light and we will join as one. If you do that each task will be achievable and the frustrations of your previous life will fall away, because you will be able to think clearly and see with such vision. As you reach higher and higher goals, well within your potential, living will seem effortless because you will be living within a new world. This world will come about, many are working for it now and the sub-planes are rising.

After the huge release of negativity from the Earth Spirit, the frequencies will start to rise. Will you rise with them, dear friends? If you wish to, we will help you. We are here, your purpose on this planet is not to suffer and struggle. The truth does not demand martyrs or sacrifice, but re-learning and re-searching. Your memories will return as you seek the life you knew before, and one truth will be known throughout Creation.

We are the Way, the Truth, and the Light. There was light, there is light now, and there shall be light forever more.

So the basic truth of Creation is now yours. I know it will challenge some people's belief, and I can understand that. We are programmed throughout our lives to limit our thinking and perceptions, because that is the best way to control us and keep us in line. We are encouraged to let 'them', the governments and institutions, do our thinking for us and tell us what we should or should not believe. But it is time to take responsibility for ourselves and stop passing it on to others. The choice is yours and yours alone. You can act upon this information, walk away or simply stand and laugh. No one in light will think any less of you whatever you do, and it is your judgement that counts.

But there are so many out there on this planet who are ready to accept and live the truth, and this is the moment for them to stand up and speak out. I can tell you from my experiences that there is no greater joy or satisfaction than seeing a life transformed by the telling of the truth. Pass on the message that will change the world. That message is: listen, people of the Earth, and open your eyes to the glorious truth. Those who see and hear will learn of the indescribable love that the Godhead has for all of us, whoever we are and whatever we do.

Let us help one another in these times of stress and change, and always remember that the truth is . . . love changes everything.

For those who wish to become involved in energy work and channelling positive energies, there is a world-wide organization called *Fountain* which is based in the United Kingdom and many other countries. They are very keen for new people to join them and work with them. The address of the UK group is:

Fountain,
PO Box 52,
Torquay,
Devon,
England,
TQ2 8PE.

Please send a stamped addressed envelope.

Also available . . .

THE TRUTH VIBRATIONS

David Icke

On 29 March 1990 David Icke visited a medium and healer. What happened that day and in the months that followed changed his life forever. The former professional footballer, TV presenter and Green politician found himself on a wondrous journey of discovery. Guided by master souls and 'extra terrestrials' from other dimensions, he went to Canada, the United States and all over Britain, meeting mediums and sensitives working on the earth's energy system.

The great mysteries which for centuries have baffled scientists, doctors and historians were explained to David Icke. Why are we here? What is the truth about God and Jesus Christ? Why are some people disabled and others not? What happens to us when we 'die'? How was the solar system formed? What are crop circles and who makes them? Who was King Arthur and what is the Holy Grail? The answers to all these questions are revealed in *The Truth Vibrations*.

Even more important, David Icke was told of what is to befall humanity in the 1990s and how we can reduce the physical and emotional impact of the enormous changes that face the planet and all life upon it. Nothing and no one will be the same again.

David Icke's astonishing story and the message *The Truth Vibrations* brings to public attention is of supreme importance to every man, woman and child on the planet.

LIVING IMAGES

Coral Polge

Coral Polge has a unique gift. While most clairvoyants describe communicators from the spirit world, she takes communications one step further and actually transmits onto paper an image of the spirit with whom she is psychically in touch, much to the amazement of the relatives of the departed.

In this updated edition of her autobiography, trained professional artist Coral Polge describes how she has come to terms with her psychic gifts. Harnessing her artistic prowess to her mediumship, she has become famous internationally for her singular talents, formerly Spiritualist of the Year and now constantly in demand all over the world.

A Londoner by birth, she tells the story of her life with honesty and humour, from an ordinary childhood background, through personal and professional progress, to her current status, ranked high in the psychic field. She does not shy away from telling of the many problems she has encountered along the way, and describes her simple and logical philosophy of how and why her gift operates.

'Seek the Truth,' Coral's spiritual guides told her in her early days. She sought and found – and now she reveals her findings which will strengthen the believers and confound the sceptics.

PSYCHICS, PROPHETS AND MYSTICS

Jon Klimo

From earliest recorded history, people have claimed that under certain special conditions they were in direct contact with, and spoke on behalf of, beings who 'inhabit a higher dimension of reality than our own'. Over the years these once ordinary people have become known by various names – spirit communicators, mediums and channels; psychics, prophets and mystics.

Those who claim to have experienced this phenomenon, the nature of the messages received, the scientific theories that explain it, and the techniques we can use to unfold our own latent capacities, are all explored in this exciting work. In addition to an in-depth historical look at cases, from the earliest recorded instances of religious revelation to centuries of underground activity, Jon Klimo reviews the principal modern channels who are bringing the messages to us and, utilizing fascinating personal interviews conducted specially for this book, he examines the current widespread popularity and acceptance of channels and mediums.

Furthermore, the book details the startling uniformity of the communications and their effect on both the 'teachers' and those who come to listen – are the messages the result of psychological disturbance or telepathy, or do other-dimensional beings really exist? More importantly, the author argues that every one of us could possess the potential to be psychics, prophets and mystics . . .

LOVE CHANGES EVERYTHING David Icke	1 85538 136 2	£4.99	☐
LIVING IMAGES Coral Polge	1 85538 084 6	£4.99	☐
PSYCHICS, PROPHETS AND MYSTICS Jon Klimo	1 85538 082 X	£7.99	☐
VISIONS OF ANOTHER WORLD Stephen O'Brien	0 85030 836 4	£4.99	☐
VOICES FROM HEAVEN Stephen O'Brien	1 85538 078 1	£4.99	☐
CONSCIOUS EVOLUTION Janet Lee Mitchell	1 85538 083 8	£5.99	☐
OUT OF MY HANDS Allon Bacon	0 85030 831 3	£6.99	☐
NOSTRADAMUS J.H. Brennan	1 85538 145 1	£4.99	☐

All these books are available at your local bookseller or can be ordered direct from the publishers.

To order direct just tick the titles you want and fill in the form below:

Name: _____

Address: _____

_____

_____ Postcode: _____

Send to: Thorsons Mail Order, Dept 3K, HarperCollins*Publishers*, Westerhill Road, Bishopbriggs, Glasgow G64 2QT.

Please enclose a cheque or postal order or debit my Visa/Access account –

Credit card no: _____

Expiry date: _____

Signature: _____

– to the value of the cover price plus:

UK & BFPO: Add £1.00 for the first book and 25p for each additional book ordered.

Overseas orders including Eire: Please add £2.95 service charge. Books will be sent by surface mail but quotes for airmail despatches will be given on request.

24 HOUR TELEPHONE ORDERING SERVICE FOR ACCESS/VISA CARDHOLDERS – TEL: **041 772 2281**.